Regional Cooking of CHINA

Margaret Gin
Alfred E. Castle

101 Productions San Francisco

1975

BOOK DESIGN: WILLIAM GIN

WOODCUTS: From the Horace Carpentier Collection,
East Asiatic Library, University of California, Berkeley

With grateful acknowledgement to Paula Lee Haller
for consultation and help in research.

Third Printing, May, 1977

Printed in the United States of America

Published by 101 Productions
834 Mission Street, San Francisco, California 94103

Distributed to the book trade in the United States by
Charles Scribner's Sons, New York, and in Canada
by Van Nostrand Reinhold Ltd., Toronto

Library of Congress Cataloging in Publication Data

Gin, Margaret, 1933–
Regional cooking of China.

Includes index.
1. Cookery, Chinese. I. Castle, Alfred, joint author. II. Title.
TX724.5.C5G5 641.5'951 75-15674
ISBN 0-912238-64-X
ISBN 0-912238-63-1 pbk.

CONTENTS

Discovering China   5
The Land and the People   7
Gods and Ghosts   13
Regional Contrasts   17
The Classic or Mandarin Cuisine   21
The Chinese Kitchen   27
Soups   33
Eggs   47
Bean Curd   57
Rice   65

Noodles   71
Vegetables   83
Seafood   101
Poultry   117
Meats   137
Dim Sum   159
Sweets   175
Glossary   178
Index   185
Biographical Notes   192

Serve foods that dazzle the eye with a thousand rainbows.
Let dishes set on the table exude myriad fragrances
Each presaging a special flavor.
Balance the yang and yin of textures
With crisp morsels, soft delicacies, sauces, soups
And the finest pearly rice.
Let lingering tastes bring only pleasant memories.
Then will a guest depart knowing he has been honored
Like a god, an emperor or a revered ancestor.

—T'sai-shuh

Discovering China

CHOLARLY GOURMETS claim the cuisine of Imperial China equals or surpasses that of the finest French chefs. *Regional Cooking of China* does not dispute this. The Classic Cuisine is described along with other fascinating aspects of China, its land, history and people.

But the world of imperial palaces, expensive restaurants and professional chefs is far removed from ordinary home kitchens and dining rooms. It is the excellence that has long existed in less pretentious surroundings that deserves "discovering."

The 18th century poet Yuan Mei, famed for his expertise in the field of food, berated the wealthy for their showy, vulgar feasts. He preached simplicity and excellence without absurd, expensive foods or cooks who fuss unnecessarily to show how clever they are. He maintained that the art of eating is open to all, that it does not take wealth to develop a discerning palate or the ingenuity to satisfy it.

As food prices soar, turning "necessities" into luxuries, one need not "eat in order to work instead of work in order to eat," in the words of Lin Yutang, the modern writer with remarkable insight into both China and America. He concludes that this is a "pretty crazy life."

The new interest in everything Chinese may have been triggered by the recent recognition of world leaders that China, after all, is part of the planet earth. But perhaps there is also another reason. People of the Western world are finding their food and energy supplies are not without limit and are seeking new ways to solve population, food and energy problems without sacrificing the "good life." They know the Chinese people have lived with shortages for centuries and somehow survived. In investigating how this was possible, many find that hidden treasures lie in the regional foods prepared in tiny Chinese kitchens. Using little meat, a wide variety of inexpensive ingredients are turned into real delicacies over small fires consuming very little energy. Home Chinese cooking turns out to be a style or an approach more than set recipes.

It's not hard to discover how the Chinese people, with minimum expense, have learned to truly enjoy eating, not merely subsist.

The Land and the People

We should pay close attention to the well-being of
the masses, from the problems of land and labour to
those of fuel, rice, cooking oil and salt.
—Mao Tse-tung, 1934

 ARCO POLO'S accounts of life in the court of Kublai Khan were largely disbelieved back in Venice when he returned around 1300 after 17 years in China. Even the fine silks, beautiful jade carvings, intricate bronze wine vessels and delicate porcelain dishes he exhibited along with the Chinese food he introduced—noodles—failed to convince many that a 3000-year-old civilization existed rivaling or surpassing that of Greece and Rome at their peaks. In Europe's eyes, China remained a remote, mythical land, generally ignored until the 1800's.

In area and latitude, China resembles the 48 United States, but here the resemblance ends. Mountains and rivers range primarily west to east, not north to south. Only 11 percent of China's area is arable compared to 80 percent in the United States, yet today its population, mostly squeezed into the eastern third of the country, is about four times that of the United States.

During the Stone Age, China's scattered river valleys and fertile plains supported pockets of agricultural civilizations largely isolated from the outside world and from each other. Later these clannish groups formed a class society, like a colorful, loosely woven patchwork quilt, that grew and prospered, bringing forth languages, inventions, philosophies, art and foods unlike anything else on the earth.

That so different a culture could develop and not spread, or even mix with those of other highly intelligent civilizations is hard to understand until a relief map of China is examined showing a rumpled terrain of river valleys and plains separated by hills and mountains. Access to the sea on the east is limited; a forbidding array of higher mountains and deserts forms an obvious barrier to the south, west and north. Provincial boundaries twist and turn with jigsaw-puzzle complexity, following natural topography rather than sightings through a surveyor's transit or the artificial lines of longitude or latitude. No wonder China's people were isolated from without and splintered within, that relatively few emigrated to other lands and that many village groups didn't even know the name of the next village. Before the advent of modern technological devices, the wonder is that Marco Polo even arrived or that any confederation or national character developed at all. In part the answer lies in the gradual peopling of river valleys and of the plains and deltas formed by the rivers as they eroded higher ground. Population pressures forced internal migration, while canals were constructed in the lowlands for transportation from one river system to another.

Surely the land itself played a major role in shaping the strong, ingrown structure of the family in which every member was ranked by age and sex. Everyone knew exactly where he stood in the family hierarchy and his relation to every other member. Girls were considered only temporary members and thus less important than boys, because they automatically were absorbed into their husband's family upon marriage. Authority increased with age just as it was assumed wisdom did. Senility or death did not end respect and veneration expected from the young and living. As the population multiplied, the "family" approach was expanded to villages, provinces and regions, creating a rigid class society that provided long periods of stability. This was a time of startling growth in the arts and sciences and material wealth during centuries when other lands were caught in whirlwinds of sweeping change, mass migration, and alternate years of flowering and devastation.

The ancient, whimsical Dragon-Kings still seem to be in charge of rainfall and rivers as cold, dry winds from the mountainous west battle moist ocean air to the east. In the winter, yellow dust blows in from the western mountains and plains as the warmth of the sea acts like a chimney. In summer, the land gets unbearably hot, and the chimney moves inland, sucking in rain-filled monsoons from the cooler sea. Normally in the north, where much of the arable land lies and the growing season is short, spring rains are light, making germination a precarious problem at best. Some years the monsoons fail to bring in sufficient summer moisture; sometimes they turn into destructive typhoons. The threat of drought or flooding, like the sword of Damocles, hangs by a hair that often breaks, bringing crop failure, famine and starvation.

The land, however, means more to the Chinese than just food. It has long played a part in mythology, poetry, art and the language. Certain mountains, lakes and rivers are revered for their special qualities. Tai-shan in northern China is not the highest mountain, but is one of the most sacred attractions because it was often visited by Confucius and many emperors. Heng Shan in Hunan Province is noted for its beauty. The Yellow River, Huang Ho, feared for its rampages, is known as the "Sorrow of China."

Written language took the form of pictures scholars used to describe the world about them. Calligraphy, an art form as well as a language, is said to include 40,000 characters, each depicting a distinct idea. Ancient manuscripts are easily read even today. The calligraphy is not phonetic, so reformers are still busy figuring new ways to record the spoken word. Of the hundred or so dialects, which are so different inter-regional communication has been almost impossible, the People's Republic has chosen to standardize on Mandarin and, as part of the "Cultural Revolution," is also working out standard Romanized spelling of the monosyllables and musical tones that combine to give meaning. This should help outsiders (who generally use tone for emphasis or to express emotion) to enjoy the brevity and subtlety of the Chinese language.

It will help them enjoy the poetry of the land, also. With even a few words such as *pei* (north), *nan* (south), *tung* (east), *hsi* (west), *ho* or *chwan* (river), *hu* (lake), *shan* (mountain) and *sze* (four), China begins to take shape. Shantung becomes "East of the Mountain"; Szechwan, "Four Rivers"; Hupei, "North of the Lake"; Hunan, "South of the Lake"; and Honan, "South of the River." Ideological place names can be more fascinating: An-hui, "Peaceful Honor"; Kan-su, "Pleasant Respect"; Fu-chien, "Prosperity Found."

Chinese civilization was born near Peking ("Northern Capital") during the third millenium B.C. in the early Stone Age. The evidence exists not in the form of monumental pyramids which were being constructed in Egypt in the same era, but in jade cut into forms of fishes. [The famous "Peking Man," an extinct Pleistocene man known from skeletal and cultural remains found in cave deposits at Choukoutien was more advanced than the "Java Man," but resembled him more than other fossil hominids and was not in any way considered "civilized."] By 2000 B.C., the early residents of China were making fine pottery, farming and raising cattle and lived in mud houses clustered in small villages protected by pounded earth walls. They were already developing a culture with government and a class society upon which the nine most famous dynasties could be said to rest. Nowhere else in the world have so many successions of family rulers dominated for so long—from 1500 B.C. to 1912 A.D., an average of about 400 years each.

This continuity had much to do with cultural and technical progress in language, the arts, scholarship and professional government. Ivory and marble sculptures, fine silks, exquisite porcelains, glazes and enamels cloisonné, tools, irrigation, paper, gunpowder, block printing and playing cards are a few of China's famous contributions to the world. The Ching Dynasty of the 1800's is credited with raising culinary arts to a peak that may never be surpassed. It provided the palace life of luxury with creative chefs in great kitchens without which, many historians avow, there can never be a truly great cuisine.

Of course, a scratch in the surface of China's glorious past would reveal ugly corruption, turmoil, cruelty and suffering at times as rulers forgot their obligation to rule justly, as invaders exploited and massacred, as nature rampaged with flood and drought. Feuding warlords vied for control and wealth, usually at the expense of peasants barely eking out a living. Some turned to opium seeking oblivion. But the resiliency of the Chinese people has always been phenomenal. Nowhere is it better demonstrated than in their ability to turn simple foods into something pleasing to eat. Some would say it's an art equal to the creation of a fine porcelain dish or a beautiful silk tapestry.

The first dynasty, Shang, ruled during the period when the family was first placed above the individual, when respect for ancestral spirits became a way of life. The time was 1500 to 1050 B.C. The emperor commanded armies in a small area of northern Honan, southern Hopeh and southwest Shantung from a central palace surrounded by houses and a mud wall. Here existed an elaborate court life. Art, pictorial writing with over 2000 characters, decorative bronze vessels, ivory and marble sculptures, daggers, axes and ritual objects of jade, elaborate harnesses and chariots represented unusual progress during what was still the Bronze Age. Spiritual power was invested in the high priest who supervised sacrifices to the deities of nature to ensure fertility and abundance. He also obtained advice from ancestors through divination of bones.

9

There followed a period of disintegration and disorder. Then in 1027 B.C., a warlike people from the northwest established the Chou Dynasty, installing their own "son of heaven" with his own "mandate from the gods." Paid officials, professional soldiers with catapults and corps of mounted archers added a new layer of social structure atop those of family and clan. Architecture added new beauty to buildings; irrigation provided some protection against the whims of nature. Feudal lords paid tribute to the new son of heaven, but otherwise did pretty much as they pleased in the villages they controlled. Serious thinkers like Confucius deliberated on the nature of man and the responsibilities of rulers. Many consider this period to be the "classical age" with its flowering of poetry, prose and art. Internal trade increased; cities were built; trade guilds and codes of law were established. Tools of iron replaced those of bronze. Money was invented. Fertilizers and the traction plow increased food production. Advanced ideas spread to the west and south.

The Ch'in Dynasty (origin of the name "China") was founded in 256 B.C. with Shih Hunag Ti becoming the first truly powerful emperor. As the "Chinese Caesar," he achieved a modicum of unity by conquering lands to the south and establishing standards of culture and commerce. During his reign, final segments of the Great Wall, that formidable 1400-mile-long barrier protecting China from barbarians to the northwest, were completed. Eight years of anarchy followed Shih's death in 210 B.C.

Establishment of the illustrious Han Dynasty in 202 B.C. led to a new era of peace and cultural development lasting until 220 A.D. The proud "Sons of Han" fought off Huns to the north, expanded westward toward Russia, then to India and Persia establishing the silk trade.

The period from 220 to 623 saw disruption and turmoil caused by invading Huns and Turks, also religious change from "invading" Buddhist pilgrims from India. When the T'ang Dynasty took over from 623 to 906, the "Sons of Han" were also proud to be known as the "Men of Tang," during what has been called the "golden era of medieval China." The Han and Tang Dynasties saw not only great expansion in scholarship, the arts and the recording of history, but also the invention of block printing, paper money and playing cards.

From 960 to 1279, the Sung Dynasty bought protection from the Tatars to the north with material goods. A good bargain for the Chinese, because during this peaceful interlude they produced the exquisite landscapes and delicate porcelains for which the dynasty is famous. In 1215, Genghis Khan, after conquering Mongolia, turned southward and sacked Peking; the Sung rulers fled to the south. But by 1279 the Mongols had destroyed the southern empire as well and went on to conquer central Asia, Persia, Mesopotamia and Europe to the Danube. China for the first time in its history was under complete foreign rule. Luckily, Genghis' successor, Kublai Khan, ruling from Peking as head of a minority group, was tolerant of Chinese culture. He encouraged drama and art and built canals, granaries and a new capital.

In 1368, in a wave of Chinese power the Mongols could not contain, a former Buddhist monk entered Peking to establish the Ming (brilliant) Dynasty which was to last until 1644. Elegant glazes and enamels cloisonnés dominated the china dishes of this period, as coloring and decoration took precedence over form. Conservative scholar rule, intellectually sterile, was re-established. Christian missionaries began to arrive from the West to convert the "heathens." The Japanese attacked, but were repulsed. European "ocean devils" sailed in to demand trade concessions. A compromise was reached with the establishment of Macao and other special trading areas, for limited trade with the outside world was considered desirable.

In 1644, descendents of Tatars previously driven off arrived on the scene to set up the Manchu, or Ching Dynasty and forced the Han people to adopt their partially shaven heads and queues considered typical of Chinese people everywhere in the 19th century. The Manchus were relatively tolerant rulers and absorbed Chinese culture, so far more advanced than their own. Yet they refused to intermarry for fear of losing their identity. As in earlier dynasties, corruption gradually ate into efficient administration and concern for the people. During the 1800's, not only was internal control deteriorating, but England, Germany, Russia, France and the United States were pressuring from without. Having surpassed China technologically, they saw China as a weak, backward nation ripe for exploitation. A great drought in 1817, growing opium addiction and a culture that stressed worship of the past did indeed make China weak. Foreigners gained control not only of the coast, but also of rivers in the interior as trading increased. Foreign courts, customs regulations and warships invaded China as surely as earlier Mongols and Tatars had, leading to the Boxer Rebellion in 1900 when patriots massacred foreigners in an abortive attempt to regain control. The United States was instrumental in establishing a "hands off" policy, partly altruistic, but also a way of keeping other predators from gaining the upper hand.

By 1912, the Manchu Dynasty was dead. Sun Yat-sen established a feeble republic dedicated to nationalism, democracy and a livelihood for all. Others tried to make it work, but China, no longer isolated, became engulfed in mighty world conflagrations. Chiang Kai-shek and Mao Tse-tung tackled China's internal problems in different ways, but united to fend off Japanese aggression during the 1930's. After World War II they parted ways and fought each other. Chiang failed on the mainland, according to some, because his approach was too similar to that of previous warlords who allowed corruption to take precedence over concern for all the people. Mao took his cue from Lenin, but added his own ideas to solve problems peculiar to China.

Today China's rulers disavow Confucian veneration of ancestors and elaborate rules of governing based on distinct levels of social strata. They hold that a peasant or factory worker deserves much the same compensation as a scholar or technical expert, that everyone's labor directed toward the common good is equally important. Mao's classless society in which all share in manual, intellectual and political labor—and in the fruits therefrom—is indeed a "great leap" away from Chinese tradition. Agronomists note that it has not yet solved China's food problems, though progress has been made. Some fear individual initiative may be stifled by a collective approach to China's long standing problems that could be as difficult as past corruption and oppression. No student of China's history, however, would discount the strength of its people to survive and continue to make major contributions of importance not just to their own lives, but to the whole world.

Gods and Ghosts

Let the Dragon King change his job,
Let the river climb the hills,
Let us ask it for 8000 acres of rice paddies.
      —Chang Chih-min, "Personalities in the Commune"

CONCEPTS like separation of Church and State, one "true" religion to the exclusion of all others, paganism, and other Western approaches categorizing various philosophies have no meaning in China. Government, language, art, the family, festivals, food, philosophy, religion and mythology all seem to be woven into a single, colorful tapestry, a kind of mystical blend of reality and fantasy about man's place in the universe.

In the Chinese pantheon, hundreds of gods and lesser personages are organized into a vast bureaucracy to run the universe with all its heavens, hells and living worlds. Since most of the gods are humans deified after death for exemplary behavior or accomplishments while on earth, it is only natural they appreciate worldly offerings of rolls of silk, disks of jade, various fruits, sweetcakes, meats and libations. They smile with favor upon earthly feasts and festivals in their honor, particularly at New Year's when all the gods descend to earth on a tour of inspection.

They control the earth and the birth, life and death of every mortal, so it is important to gain and hold their good will—from the Four Dragon-Kings in charge of distributing by region the life-giving rains or death-dealing floods, to lesser Dragon-Kings controlling individual rivers, streams and wells; from the trio Lu-hsing, Fu-hsing and Shou-hsing, the gods of salaries, happiness and long life (or early death) respectively, to Ts'ai-shen, the god of wealth who likes sacrifices of cocks and living carps; from the lowly door gods that keep the dead from coming back to harm the living, to the mighty sovereign of them all, the August Personage of Jade, Yu-ti.

It was to Yu-ti that emperors with great pomp and pageantry would make solemn sacrifices of silk, jade, meats and wine at the huge Temple of Heaven just south of Peking, first at the winter solstice, then again in the spring. It is Yu-ti who allots annual quotas of happiness or misfortune to every household in China.

Since the August Personage of Jade can't possibly attend to all the details of the universe, he assigns certain functions to various departments, ministers and subordinates. All must turn in reports to keep him informed. Each family well knows their Kitchen God, Tsao-wang, is charged with reporting their doings personally to Yu-ti at the end of the year and then receives their allotment of sorrow and joy for the year to come. He has been observing them from his paper picture above the hearth and knows them well. As he leaves on the 23rd of the twelfth month, his mouth is stuffed with sweets to induce him to say sweeter things about the family. Since the journey to the highest heaven is long and arduous, extra food for him and straw for his horse are given in offering. Firecrackers are touched off to boost him on his way. Then his picture is burned on a small fire of pine twigs. On New Year's, Tsao-wang returns. Another sacrifice is made; firecrackers burst high in the air help him find the right hearth; a new picture is hung.

Far away at the center of the earth atop K'un-lun Mountain, Yu-ti's wife, Hsi Wang Mu, the Lady-Queen of the West, reigns supreme. She dwells in a nine-story jade palace surrounded by magnificent gardens and the renowned Imperial Orchard, where P'an-t'ao, the Peaches of Immortality, ripen every 3000 years. Occasionally a human being is allowed to eat the peach, the sign of longevity, during his stay on earth, but the peach is usually reserved for great banquets of the immortals, presided over by the Lady-Queen.

In a separate world with towns and country lies the land of the Yama Kings with its 18 hells. Ox-head and Horse-face collect dying souls on earth and bring them here. Since they occasionally make mistakes and a soul is permitted to return, burial is best postponed, sometimes as long as 49 days.

Bad souls on arrival may be cut to bits, re-assembled, boiled in oil, restored and so on, progressing through enough hells to atone for earthly sins. Then they are ready to appear before the Tenth Yama King (of the Wheel of Transmigration) for a ruling on how they will be reborn. Pleasant possibilities include becoming a god, a good demon (not as pleasant) or another human, which could be most unpleasant if a man were to be reborn as a beggar, an invalid or a woman. Disagreeable fates would include remaining as a permanent resident of hell, becoming a starving demon, or returning to earth as an animal with human thoughts and feelings, but no way to express them. All souls are fed the Broth of Oblivion before rebirth.

A soul arriving in hell not deserving torture might go immediately to Buddha in the Land of Extreme Felicity in the West, the place of all delights far beyond an infinity of worlds like our own. Or a soul may go directly to the Tenth Yama King. The highest honor, though, would be immediate assignment to the Mountain K'un-lun to dine on the Peaches of Immortality and live with the gods.

Confucius, Siddhartha Gautama and Lao-tzu, those three great contemplators of man's nature and his relation to others and the world about him, all lived around 500 B.C. Since all three were deeply concerned with the good life for all and tried to exemplify what they preached in their own lives, they would probably accept deification as natural after death, even though none claimed to be more than a simple human being. That their followers expanded their simple ideas into the elaborate religions of Confucianism, Buddhism and Taoism with beautiful temples, often shared, might have surprised them. But they would surely deplore all of the absurdities, cruelties and inhibiting extremes of the powerful imposed on the people in their names.

Confucius believed in the class society, that the better life could come only by organization, respect for the past and good rules of living together. The people would be good if the rulers took care of the people, set a good example and governed fairly while the people expanded their knowledge. Unscrupulous rulers during the 18th century did much to stifle China's growth by twisting respect for the past into worship, by turning the class society into a nightmare of the very rich and the very poor.

Lao-tzu, the founder of Taoism, proclaimed that people are good if left alone and if they live close to nature, letting the senses, not the intellect, drink in the good life. Buddha (meaning to become enlightened), as Siddhartha Gautama became named, taught that suffering is caused by evil desire for pleasure that makes men slaves of material things. Love, not selfishness, would lead to a heaven on earth of perfect insight: nirvana, a quality of mind.

Bits and pieces of these basically simple philosophies have long since been woven into the great fabric of mysticism. Statues of Buddha proliferated almost as fast as the people themselves. To a Taoist, foods and medicines, one and the same, were considered the primary nourishment of the mind as well as the body. Eating strange fruits and vegetables, especially fresh lotus seeds with delicate flavor born of the dew, was pure poetry. If he could, a Taoist would drink the dew.

Confucians venerating their ancestors selected tombs and burial times with the help of professionals. Late in the second month favorite foods, wine and flowers were offered at Ch'ing Ming, the Festival of the Sweeping the Tombs. Later, on the 15th of the seventh month, came the Feast of the Hungry Ghosts with offerings of fish, eggs, pork, cabbage, rice, wine and money to appease spirits of ancestors not properly worshipped throughout the year.

In the spring came the great festival Li Ch'un, the Beating of the Ox, when the Emperor would plow the first furrow. Confucians had their God of the Soil, whose two associates were the Gods of Ploughing and the Harvest. Peasants worshipped Hou Chi (Prince Millet), Celestial Prince Liu (Superintendent of the Five Cereals) and Hu-shen, who sends the hail or protects against it. The God of Cattle Breeding had two special aides, the King-of-Oxen and the Transcendent Pig.

In China spirits were ever present. Food was as important to the gods and ghosts as it was to the living during festivals scattered throughout the year—Feast of Lanterns, Festival of Flowers, Dragon Boat Festival, Festival of the August Moon (for females only), Festival of All Souls, to name but a few. On Buddhist "holy" days, artful vegetarian dishes resembling meat or fish lived up to the letter if not the spirit of abstinence from eating living creatures. However, some Chinese believe that oysters are so necessary to their dishes that Buddha himself declared the oyster was not an animal, but a plant.

Regional Contrasts

DMINISTRATIVELY, China today comprises 29 divisions of the first order—21 provinces, five autonomous regions and three municipalities (Peking, Shanghai and Tientsin). Along with other major cities, each offers its food specialties, but, to bring some order out of delightful chaos, food scholars generally categorize Chinese cooking into four major styles primarily based on climate, temperament of the people and foods generally available in quantity. Since the styles are variously identified by cities, provinces and autonomous regions, it helps to list all three designations, when applicable.

NORTH EAST
Cities: Peking, Tientsin
Provinces: Hopei, Shantung,
Shansi, Shensi, Honan
Regions: Inner Mongolia, Manchuria

EAST
Cities: Shanghai, Ning-po, Hangchow,
Fuchow, Nanking, Amoy
Provinces: Kiangsu, Anwei,
Chekiang, Kiangsi, Fukien

SOUTH EAST
Cities: Canton (Hongkong, Macao)
Province: Kwantung
Regions: Kwangsi Chuang, Hai-nan Island

SOUTH WEST
Cities: Chengtu, Chungking
Provinces: Szechwan, Hunan,
Hupeh, Kweichow, Yunnan

The North East is often associated with the Classic or Mandarin Cuisine, because Peking has historically usually been the home of whatever centralized government existed. But the tremendous imperial kitchens rarely depended only on foods generally available in this region of cold dry winters, instant springs and hot summers. More characteristic of North Eastern regional cooking is the generally limited variety of ingredients available in an area with a rather dry, short growing season: soybeans, wheat, millet and kaoliang (sorghum). Rice was a luxury in the north. But there were the meat products of grazing animals of the nomads to the north, also vegetables like cabbage, carrots, turnips, spinach, scallions and garlic, and of course the ubiquitous chickens, ducks and pork.

Manchu stews, roasts and barbecues very definitely belong to the North East, even though frowned upon by many of the Han Chinese majority who prefer less "barbaric" foods like wheat noodles, steamed bread and buns, along with chicken with chestnuts or cold jellied pork. Seasoning of this region is generally mild, sauces tend to be rich. A substantial Moslem minority eats lamb, while others enjoy pork in addition to fat ducks and plump fish. The fish come from the meandering river called Yellow because it is loaded with silt from its rampaging upper reaches, the famous yellow loesslands. Wheat flour may go into *paotse*, steamed buns filled with pork or pork fat; *laoping*, thick wheat cakes in which are wrapped scallions or garlic; or *jao-tze*, a paste-like ravioli filled with raw lamb or pork to be boiled, fried or steamed. Fried bean curd is served with salty, sour, aromatic sauce. Preserved meats, fruits and vegetables in earthenware jars have long helped carry families through the long months when fresh foods are scarce.

Shanghai, like Peking, developed a reputation for haute cuisine, for it not only inherited court life driven southward during times of strife in the north, but was protected by distance from the "barbarian" influence of Mongolian people. In later years it was to become more cosmopolitan than Peking, for as a seacoast city it was influenced by more contact with the foods of the rest of the world. But it's not this influence Westerners are most intrigued with. It's the fish and the seafood of the area, the shad, mullet and perch of the lakes, rivers, canals and ocean; the juicy dainty buns and fancy appetizers the brown stock sauce used over and over that imparts the same yet different flavor to many foods as each use adds a little something new; the fancy slivered bean curds. Fish are often roasted, then fried till the bones are brittle enough to be chewed, not picked out. The foods become heterogeneous to an extreme, almost too fancy, with too many mixtures instead of individual flavors. Yet individual specialties have become famous like eel in gravy, pigs' knuckles and a unique version of bird's nest soup. No one disputes the excellence of Fukien soy sauce, the vinegar and ham from Chekiang, the wine, noodles, and pastries of the Eastern provinces. Shanghai's elaborate braised meats rich with gravy and soy sauce are often cooked with pickled or salted greens. Rice, as a staple, absorbs strong flavors. Stir-frying is comparatively slow and long; casseroles are cooked long, too.

Fukien and Amoy to the south are sometimes classed as a separate cuisine because the area is relatively isolated from the cities to the north like Shanghai on the coast and Nanking inland. Here more seafoods abound—oysters, clams and more fish—along with many clear soups. According to some, this area's soy sauce is the very best and is used unsparingly. Wines are used subtly in cooking; the fermented rice paste is superb.

The milder, moister South East with its more fertile land vegetation has always offered a wider variety of ingredients to the skillful Cantonese cook. There was less need to disguise or modify flavors to stimulate palates bored by the same old food day after day. Here the Taoist idea of enjoying foods in their natural state could be a real joy, as could Buddhist vegetarianism. Rice was a staple, not a luxury. Fresh foods, available year round, needed only light soy and few seasonings to enhance their natural flavor. Cooking was more casual, involving coarser cutting and chopping, with lots of quick stir-frying that left ingredients full of color, crisp and tender. Here exotic ingredients abounded, too, one of the most famous being shark's fin.

Being near the sea and far from the inhibiting influence of Peking, the Cantonese in the 16th century were the first to establish substantial contacts with other peoples. They quickly added corn, tomatoes, peanuts, and French pastries to their fare.

Fresh ginger root, wine, sugar, and chicken broth are more extensively used in South East cooking than elsewhere. Here the *jao-tze*, the ravioli-like pastes, are smaller and may be filled with prawns, bamboo shoots or mushrooms. Those delightful dumplings and buns filled with meat, seafood, or sweetened bean mixtures—dim sum—are eaten any time of the day or night. There are numerous steamed pork and chicken dishes; sweet and sour pork has long been known and liked around the world. Much seafood is available along the coast—shrimp, oysters, crab, lobsters, snails, octopus and squid as well as fish. Roast Cantonese duck is quite different from Peking duck, that most classic of foods in the Mandarin cuisine. Barbecued spareribs, pork strips, or whole roast pig are unsurpassed when seasoned in the Cantonese style.

Last, but not least, come the unforgettable foods of the South West. For some, their first taste of fiery Szechwan cooking will be their last. If they reach for a water glass to put out the fire in their mouths and throats, they'll find it's like putting out a bonfire with gasoline. The flames just leap higher.

At first taste this brilliant freak among Chinese cuisines appears to break all the rules. But those who do not pursue it will never discover its spectrum of flavors—sour, salty, sweet, fragrant, bitter, and hot—that can be tasted all at once after the shock that doesn't really paralyze the palate (as long as water is avoided), but rather stimulates the taste buds. The hot introduction is followed by a kind of mellowness produced by somewhat oily, yet dry and chewy textures. One can not gulp this kind of food; he savors it slowly, and enjoys the lingering aftertastes, too.

That South West cooking is so different is attributed not only to its hot climate where "hot" foods predominate, but also to the isolation of an ancient kingdom that developed in the Chengtu Plain, a protected fertile triangle on the upper headwaters of the mighty Yangtze River and its four tributaries, protected from cold winter winds and summer typhoons by three mountain ranges and their huge cliffs. This is a subtropical area where rice and bamboo and tea abound, and year-round agriculture produces dry grains in the winter and wet rice in the summer. Paper-wrapped chicken, steamed pork, vegetables cooked in chicken fat, chicken skin in rich stock, sour and hot soup, gourds, marrows and cucumbers—all liberally spiced with red and green peppers, crushed wild peppercorns, sesame seeds and the bark of the cassia trees (cinnamon)—perk up the spirits during very hot summers and throughout the year. Dumplings are made "inside out" by rolling sesame seed filling in flour. *Jao-tze* are filled with pork and cabbage and served with three separate sauces —mix-your-own style—red pepper oil, concentrated soy sauce and scallion paste. Mushrooms are used not only with vegetables, but also in desserts. It was probably here that peaches achieved their legendary role as symbols of immortality. Fresh water seafoods are more available in Hupeh and Hunan farther down the Yangtze on the east.

It would be a mistake to assume that the four regions mentioned are still separate and distinct in their styles of cooking, for over the years there has occurred a gradual intermingling of ideas with better transportation and communication. So many adaptations, variations and modifications have sprung up that origins of specific foods have been forgotten. Yet exploring regional differences can be a fascinating pastime.

The Classic or Mandarin Cuisine

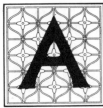S FAR BACK as 500 B.C., government officials, poets, philosophers, artists and emperors considered themselves to be connoisseurs and critics of fine food. Ancient writings include those of many articulate gourmets who expounded at length on glorious feasts. Confucius is said to have divorced his wife for failure in good cooking—or she fled because "rice could never be white enough, or mincemeat could never be chopped fine enough, or meat was not in the proper sauce or not cut square or the color was not right."

By the second century A.D., opulence among the upper classes extended to the dining room, and the Classic Cuisine was born, with over 9,000 characters in script designating foods, cooking methods and utensils. By the eighth century it had developed a distinct pattern and style, but it was to reach its zenith around 1800. This was the time the poet Yuan Mei wrote volumes about food which are still considered to be definitive studies of Chinese gourmet cooking in the Mandarin style. This cuisine included the best ingredients and dishes of all regions and encompassed many "rustic" or peasant foods looked upon as chic by the wealthy.

The combining of flavors, aromas and textures was studied as diligently as art forms on canvass or silk or in sculpture, sometimes to the point of absurdity. Yuan maintained that flavors should be either rich and robust but never oily, or delicate and fresh without being too thin. To those who liked greasy food he suggested dining on lard, intimating that some of the effete food snobs he preached against might do just that.

When a host wished to entertain at home rather than in an expensive restaurant, he would hire a professional chef, if there was none on his permanent staff. The chef would plan the entire feast in meticulous detail and personally purchase only the freshest, best and rarest ingredients without regard to cost. He would arrive with his own elaborate equipment often including special stoves, together with a retinue of assistants. With the eye of an eagle he would oversee the washing, slicing, chopping, marinating, preliminary mixing and firing up of hearth and stove without once lifting a finger to help. Then only he would perform the final steps: the crucial combining of flavor, texture and color; the quick, high-heat cooking that sealed in goodness and left foods crisp with natural color, or the carefully controlled steaming or dry baking at a slower pace; the artistic arranging of foods designed to please the eye before titillating the palate.

No one questioned his menu or disputed his methods, for he was a true artist. For a guest to be displeased was inconceivable. At least this was the way things were supposed to be. But food was a serious matter, and as Yuan Mei put it, "If one does not keep the cook in line, he becomes insolent." Everyone at the table was expected to analyze in detail the good and bad points of every dish. If a food was good, all were expected to let the chef know why. If deficient, he was told how it could be improved.

One writer records that the 18th century emperor Chien Lung in his travels encountered in a small city an appetizing dish he was told was "Red-Beaked Green Parrot with Gold Trimmed Jade Cake." Actually it was made cheaply with red-rooted green spinach and fried bean curd, ingredients thought to be too humble for the royal palate. On returning to Peking, Chien Lung ordered his head chef to serve this dish. Neither the chef nor his assistants had ever heard of it; all were puzzled. But the chef purchased, slaughtered, cooked and served a parrot along with a piece of jade. Chien Lung, his appetite spoiled, had the chef beheaded.

That the Classic Cuisine reached elaborate, imaginative extremes to the point of absurdity can best be demonstrated by the menu of an 18th century banquet (reproduced below) reported by Yuan Mei with the following commentary.

"Nowadays, at the start of a feast, the menu is about a hundred feet long and there are many dishes and bowls on the table. This is merely display, not gastronomy. Official circles favor the 16-8-4 [16 hors d'oeuvre, 8 entrées, 4 important dishes] or the Great Chinese Banquet."

Bird's Nest Soup
Slices of Unicorn
Cassia Flowers on a Moonlit Boat
Roast Whole Suckling Pig
Deer Heart Garnished with Plums
Lady's Grace
Fish Maw with Six Spices
Deer Tail with Clams and Duck
Dragon Liver and Phoenix Marrow (chicken liver and brains)
Chicken Testicles
Whole Squabs, Garnished
Seal
Clam Cakes
Phoenix Bursting through the Clouds (cold plate)
Delicacies from Sung River
Jade on a Blue Field
Sautéed Shark's Fins
A Pair of Nanking Ducks
Sparrows and Pine Nuts
Deep-Fried Lobster Balls
Frogs

etc.

Another excellent description of the great Mandarin banquets is the on-the-scene report of an Englishman, Ch. H. Eden, published in 1880:

"The empty sides of the table where no one sat were hung with scarlet drapery, beautifully worked in embroidery of gold and different colored silks. On the front edge of each table were placed the finest fruits in little baskets, with beautiful flowers stuck between them. Besides these the whole table was covered with little cups and plates, which were ranged with great precision, and contained fruits, preserves, confectionery, slices of bread and butter, with small birds cold, and hundreds of other things. An extraordinary degree of art had been expended in the arrangement of those articles; amongst the rest were whole rows of little plates filled with elegantly-raised three- and four-cornered pyramids, composed of little bits of pheasant, larded geese, sausages, and so forth. Here stood plates of small oranges; there, preserved plums; and here again, almonds. Various little seeds of different colors were served upon shallow saucers, so arranged, however, that each color occupied a particular field. There were quince seeds, of very delicate flavor, chick peas, chestnuts and hazel nuts; also preserved ginger, citron, and lemon.

"By way of cover, three small cups are placed before each seat; the first, on the left, is filled with soya sauce, which the Chinese add to almost every sort of food; the second serves for ordinary eating; and in the third is a little spoon of porcelain for the soups. In front of these three cups, which are arranged in a line, lie two round ivory chop-sticks.

"As soon as the first course was removed, another small cup was added to each cover, to be used for drinking hot rice wine, offered by servants walking round with large silver cans.

"So soon as the first division of the dinner, consisting possibly of 60 ragouts, was over, the soups appeared; these were placed in small bowls in the middle of the table, and everyone ate, with his little porcelain spoon, out of the dish. In this way five or six different soups were served in succession, and between them various other things were placed before the guests in little cups; amongst these, pastry prepared in many ways, articles of confectionery, and strong chicken-hashes. Between the different grand divisions of the dinner, tea was handed round, and tobacco was smoked.

"After several more courses, five small tables were placed outside of the half-circle of original tables; these were completely covered with roasted pork and birds of all sorts. Then ten cooks came into the room, clothed all alike and very tastefully, and began carving the roasts. Other servants, who stood in front of the tables, received the little bits upon small plates, and then placed them on the dining tables, to complete the repast."

At its extreme the Classic Cuisine involved several days of continuous feasting, yet wines were used only sparingly to enhance the food and conviviality. Wheat, millet, or rice wines were the primary cooking wines. At the table or on other special occasions, orange, pear, fruit rinds and herb, celery, rose, citron or kaoliang (sorghum) wines might be served, though kaoliang wine in reality was a liquor similar to gin. Just as Yuan Mei deplored over-elaborate foods, he warned against excessive use of spirits, for "Only a sober man can distinguish good flavors from bad. Words are inadequate to describe various shades of taste. How much less then must a stuttering sot be able to appreciate them." Grape wines were seldom mentioned, but it is recorded that the emperor in 1322 decreed the destruction of all vineyards, whether for puritanical or other reasons is not known. Vineyards and grape wines have gradually reappeared since.

The great feasts of the Classic Cuisine involving style, form and rhythm like a grand symphony involved so much time, labor, thought and money that these banquets more or less toppled from favor from their own weight. Even the wealthy sought relief from satiety in simpler foods like plain rice, bean curd, vegetables, congees and uncomplicated soups. Remnants of this grandiose approach—delicious, rare, complicated and very expensive—can still be found on menus of fine restaurants or be specially ordered by those who can afford them, but of more interest to the home cook are the food philosophy and concepts of the Classic Cuisine purged of their absurdities by critics like Yuan Mei.

The duality of nature emphasizing contrasts, and the golden mean epitomizing harmony and balance, are considered important in food as well as other aspects of life. The Mystic Dual Principle called Yang-Yin represents the interaction of opposites in nature which, when united, produce benevolence, purity, propriety, wisdom and truth. Yang comprises Heaven, Sun, Light, Vigor, Male, Penetration, Azure Color, Mountains and Odd Numbers. Yin takes in the Earth, Moon, Dark, Quiescence, Female, Absorption, Valleys and Even Numbers. The egg is considered the perfect embodiment of Yang and Yin with its white and yolk enclosed in one shell, yet distinct and separate. In the 11th century a poet named Su-Tung-Po went into ecstasies analyzing the egg's intricate structure in a long treatise, and great care went into cooking it to perfection.

Critics developed a special vocabulary and sets of rules about food far more complex than in any other part of the world. At times they delighted in a cook's trickery when he converted commonplace ingredients into something new and better with no natural flavors. At other times they demanded that the cook carefully preserve natural flavors while he blended, mixed, matched or contrasted recognizable ingredients. The trickery here involves subtly enhancing natural flavors with scallions, garlic, light soy, salt, sugar, wine or vinegar. Scallions and garlic are removed before serving; extra wine or vinegar is evaporated; other seasonings are used so sparingly their presence can not be detected. Then if complementary or contrasting flavors are desired they appear openly at the table in the form of separate, special sauces.

Flavors and fragrance are like pitch and tone to a composer. If similar, they are blended; if contrasting, they are matched. Bad flavors are converted by cooking or changed with seasoning. Foods rich in flavor combine well with "texture" foods of little taste. Indiscriminate mixtures are no more tolerated than discordant musical chords.

The "soul" of a food is its *hsien* (sweet natural flavor) and *hsiang* (aroma). Both are treated with reverence. *Hsien* can sometimes be simulated, but never *hsiang,* for it is contained in the basic oils of foods like onions, chicken fat, or mushrooms to be released in cooking.

Nung is the rich, concentrated flavor essence of meats and spices that might be overpowering unless handled with care. The taste (but not the oiliness) of fat as found in well-cooked pork belly, *yu-er-pu-ni,* complements other tastes. Textures, either natural or built in by the cook, include: *tsuei,* the crisp crunchiness of pork cracklings or skin of a Peking duck; *nun,* soft, tender, non-fibrous resiliency; and *ruan,* the soft, loose texture of a perfect soft-boiled egg or chicken meat whose fibers have been destroyed and reconstituted into velvet chicken.

Both critic and cook know that all of these qualities can be enjoyed separately or, with no contradiction, together in all possible combinations.

Dozens of terms describe cooking methods. *Ch'ao* (high heat, little oil, open wok) and *shao* ("red cooking," or stewing with soy sauce) are universal. Others describe regional specialties. North China has its *lao* (dry grilling in a skillet as used for wheat flour cakes). A favorite in Shanghai is *tun* (covered-pot stewing). *Pien* (dry stir-frying) and *yen* (soaking and steeping of vegetables) come from Szechwan.

Manipulating food with chopsticks in an expert manner is naturally expected both in the kitchen and at the table, but the gourmet is also expected to master the art of manipulating food properly in his mouth with tongue and teeth. To merely masticate and swallow is considered as vulgar as gulping a goblet of wine. The tongue and teeth have to learn to slowly savor every texture while making sure every taste bud has its chance to enjoy all the flavors before delicacies are reluctantly relinquished to a stomach asking only to be filled with digestible nourishment.

All foods are expected to be tasted, but only children (seated at a separate table) are expected to finish everything set before them. There are always many hungry mouths behind the scenes to consume what is left on the platter or in the bowl. At the very least there will be a clever cook who can concoct new creations out of the surplus.

Pies are cooked of millet and bearded maize.
Guests watch the steaming bowls
And sniff the pungency of peppered herbs.
The cunning cook adds slices of bird-flesh,
Pigeon and yellow-heron and black crane.

Next are brought
Fresh turtle, and sweet chicken cooked with cheese
Pressed by the men of Ch'u
And flesh of whelps floating in liver sauce
With salad of minced radishes in brine;
All served with that hot spice of southern wood
The land of Wu supplies.
          —Ch'u Yuan, Third century B.C.

The Chinese Kitchen

Traditional Chinese cooks might find a book of specific recipes and detailed directions rather baffling and confining, for most of them learn how to prepare food by first watching others and imitating, then improvising on their own with ingredients at hand. To them cooking is more a matter of approach and methods than following recipes. The dishes explicitly described in *Regional Cooking of China* should therefore be considered starting points subject to many variations. General comments on the Chinese approach may help a newcomer feel at home.

INGREDIENTS

In Chinese cooking, meat is a luxury to be used sparingly, usually in small pieces mixed with other foods. Dairy products are practically non-existent. Fruits and vegetables are elevated to new heights of importance.

Some people are repelled by ingredients that seem strange, smell bad, look odd or are tasteless by themselves, but it should be remembered that cooking, combining and seasoning can work miracles.

This does not mean, however, that poor quality in ingredients can be overlooked or covered up. Dried, fermented or other preserved foods processed by experts usually present no problems, but the freshness of meats, fruits and vegetables is a cook's responsibility. Chinese markets throughout the world take pride in freshness. They know they must in order to retain their Oriental customers. Chickens are often trucked in live and butchered at the last minute. Some markets even have tanks of live fish. Vegetables are displayed openly to be picked over by cooks who know a tired old cabbage will never have the texture or flavor it should, whether stir-fried or served raw.

Fresh fruits might be considered the "candy bars" of China. Their sweetness has always been enjoyed between meals, and, although Chinese meals rarely have desserts, fruits can add a refreshing note at the end of a typical dinner. The historical importance of fruits is typified by the peach as the symbol of longevity and the pomegranate with its many seeds as the symbol of fertility. Oranges invariably appear at New Year's. Colors are described as apricot, citron, persimmon and tangerine.

SLICING, DICING, MATCHSTICK CUTTING, SLIVERING, SHREDDING AND MINCING

With only soup spoons and chopsticks on the Chinese table instead of an array of knives and forks, it naturally follows that all necessary cutting is done ahead of time in the kitchen, and that there are no spreads to be applied to breads. Beside making food manipulable with chopsticks, cutting ingredients into bite-size or smaller pieces beforehand enhances the cooking process in several ways. Small pieces have more surface area exposed to heat and seasonings; cooking is quicker requiring less fuel. Chopsticks may be used for high heat stir-frying that immediately seals in crispness and flavor. Ingredients requiring different degrees of cooking can be added at different times.

How to cut depends on the inherent cooking needs and texture of each ingredient, as well as the desired role it is to play in the finished dish. Generally, uniform sizes in a single serving bowl make for easier eating and a sense of harmony; variety is provided by interspersing dishes using sliced ingredients with other dishes having diced, shredded or minced contents. Often the dominant-texture food determines how others will be cut. Bean sprouts call for slivers; peas for diced meats; bamboo shoots for slices.

Together with a heavy, solid chopping block, the razor-sharp Chinese cleaver is ideal not only for cutting, but also chopping bones, smashing garlic and ginger, tenderizing meat with the blunt edge, scaling fish, skinning, and transporting foods to the stove. The cleaver is an awesome tool. Apprentice chefs in China spend hours mastering all the intricacies of its use by observation and practice, but even beginners find it handy. Though a heavy chef's knife can be used in place of a cleaver, manipulating it will prove no less dangerous, and the cleaver is more versatile on a chopping block. The secret in cutting is to hold food down with the left hand in a loose fist with the knuckles against the side of the blade. Then if you never lift the blade higher than the knuckles, they will keep the blade in position and fingers out of harm's way. Grasping a cleaver is not like holding a hatchet or a slim knife. Its broad blade requires "rotational" control, which is accomplished by placing the thumb and forefinger on either side of the blade while the other fingers hold the handle. Mincing is especially easy as the left hand holds the end of the blade down on the block and the right hand rocks the cleaver down and up in a fast rhythm.

Cutting is rather complicated and therefore more interesting. *Slicing,* for example, can be straight, diagonal or angle cut. Straight, vertical slicing is appropriate for soft foods like mushrooms. Fibrous foods like celery and some meats call for diagonal cutting to de-emphasize stringiness. The angle cut produces interesting geometrical chunks with maximum surface area by making a series of 30-degree cuts as the food is rolled on the block. It is good for cylindrical vegetables like carrots, Chinese okra and turnips that require longer cooking.

Dicing is best approached by first cutting foods into long strips with a square cross section, then slicing vertically. *Cubes* (1/2 to 2 inches) are for slow cooking or deep-frying; *dice* (1/8 to 1/2 inch) for stir-frying.

Matchstick cutting produces long, narrow sticks or strips about 1/8 inch thick, much like what the French call julienne. *Slivering* denotes short, thin, narrow strips. *Shredding* varies with the type of food. Cooked meats are torn apart with the fingers with the grain of the meat to form strings. Vegetables such as cabbage are shredded by slicing very thinly into long strands.

Mincing is chopping very finely. Round balls of minced ingredients are prized as symbols of "togetherness." Minced foods generally are steamed. If garlic and ginger are to be widely distributed yet retain their identity, they should be minced, not smashed.

THE WOK

Along with the firepot and bamboo steamer, the wok is truly an ingenious cooking device. Its wide spherical shape permits cooking large or small quantities with much or little oil. Its rounded surface distributes heat efficiently and permits stir-frying bulky items without danger of spilling. It comes with a single wooden handle or double ones of metal, with or without cover and ring base. The single wooden handle eliminates the need for a pot holder and can be held with one hand. On the other hand, the double metal-handled wok is not so hazardous, requires less storage space and can be used in the oven or over charcoal. Use of the ring base depends on the type of stove. Some woks have a flatter bottom; these are steadier and better suited for use on electric stoves.

Any metal pan used for high-heat cooking needs "seasoning," because metals are porous. Minute food particles may be trapped and cause sticking. To season a new wok, first wash thoroughly with detergent and hot water to remove objectionable oils and dirt remaining from the manufacturing process. Rinse well and dry over heat. Rub inside with peanut oil and place over high heat for 1 minute. Rinse in hot water and dry over heat. Repeat the process several times, never using detergents, for they would remove the hardened oil that is gradually filling in the metal's pores. Now the wok is ready for initial use, but the seasoning process continues provided detergents and scouring pads are never used to make it gleam like new and re-open the pores. Cleaning should never exceed the application of hot water and a stiff brush followed by drying over heat to prevent rust.

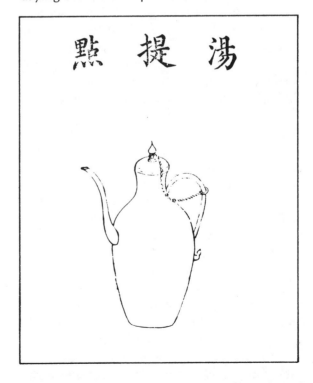

STIR-FRYING

Considered to be the key to many successful Chinese dishes, stir-frying is more than indiscriminately tossing foods into a wok partially filled with hot oil then stirring with chopsticks. You have to know what you're doing and watch the wok closely.

First, heat the wok (or large, heavy frying pan) over very high heat until a drop of water will sizzle. Then add oil (peanut oil is most commonly used, though corn oil may be substituted) and heat it until it just begins to smoke. Next, add ingredients to flavor the oil, such as ginger, garlic and chili peppers, stir-frying constantly for a few seconds to release their essence. Add the remaining ingredients in order of their required cooking time. Stir-fry the meat first and remove it from the pan. Add and cook the vegetables, the coarser ones first, then the more delicate ones. Return the meat to the wok with the vegetables to just heat through. Add the liquid seasonings, such as soy sauce, in a swirling motion, blending in well to coat all of the ingredients thoroughly. It is important that the ingredients be cooked quickly and receive even heat. This seals in the juices of the meat and ensures the crispness and vibrant color of the vegetables. With efficient stir-frying, flavors are combined without the loss of identity of the individual ingredients.

STEAMING

The multi-layered bamboo steamer atop a wok of gently boiling water can steam foods to perfection. If you don't have a steamer, steaming can be done in a dish suspended above boiling water in a large, covered vessel.

This is quite different from a double boiler, which merely controls temperature. A proper platform to hold the cooking dish should be high enough so that bubbling water does not splash into the food. Expandable steamer racks make excellent platforms; or racks may be improvised by cutting out both ends of a small can, such as a tuna fish can.

SERVING

Typically, the Chinese home table is set with only individual chopsticks, rice bowls and porcelain soup spoons with occasional small containers for special sauces. The table is round for easy access to the communal soup bowl in the center, around which other dishes are arranged. Unlike a Chinese banquet, at home all foods are usually served at once to be partaken at random. Though the communal soup bowl is traditional, individual soup bowls are often preferred today.

Even left-handed children are made to eat with their right hand. All develop proficiency with chopsticks at an early age. Chopsticks come in various shapes and sizes, in bamboo, wood, ivory, coral, jade and now in plastic. To avoid them is to miss much of the fun of Chinese dining. With a bowl of rice held close to the mouth, they function almost like a shovel, but more skill is required to deliver other morsels, especially slippery peas. Their secret lies in holding the lower chopstick stationary and separately in a "tripod" consisting of the crotch between thumb and forefinger, the base of the thumb and the tip of the third finger. This leaves the tips of the thumb and first two fingers free to hold the other chopstick like a pencil parallel to the stationary chopstick and hopefully manipulate it so the two tips are in close enough proximity to grasp food. At first, lack of control can be as hilarious as crossed skis on a snow slope, but with a little perseverance anyone can learn to enjoy Chinese food untainted with the metallic taste of a fork.

When entertaining, table settings may be more elaborate and there may be too many dishes to permit serving all at once. However, there is no main course or set sequence of serving the many main dishes that appear, except perhaps to group them into complementing and contrasting varieties.

MENU PLANNING

Of the reams that have been written about planning a Chinese menu, most apply to feasts, not to the simple, economical, yet delicious meals served in Chinese homes. The size of the recipes in this book are based on the following formula. For four, a meal should probably consist of a soup, a poultry, seafood or meat dish including other ingredients as well, a vegetable dish and, of course, steamed rice. For five or six, another dish would be added, and so on.

When planning what to serve, two things should be considered. First, the dishes must complement one another. For a Chinese meal, this means a contrasting of flavors, colors, textures and aromas. Second, for the ease of the cook, the dishes planned should utilize different means of cooking—stir-frying, steaming, roasting, etc.—so that they may be served as nearly as possible at the same time.

Generally there are only two main meals a day in a Chinese household—late morning and early evening—with treats like fresh fruits or pastries in between. Contrary to popular belief, tea is not always an integral part of meals. It has been more a beverage to be sipped off and on throughout the day like water, and its popularity developed to a large extent because of medicinal virtues and scarcity of pure water. However, most will agree a good tea makes a pleasing adjunct to a Chinese meal.

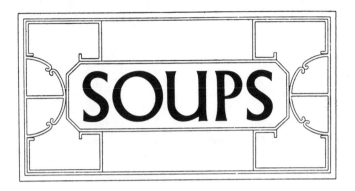

SOUPS

BASIC RICH CHICKEN STOCK

1 3-pound chicken*, cut in quarters, or
3 pounds chicken backs, necks and wings
1 slice ginger root
1 tablespoon salt
8 cups water

Combine ingredients in soup kettle, bring to boil and skim off any scum that rises to top. Lower heat to simmer, cover and cook slowly 3 hours. Cool the chicken in the broth and then remove chicken. Strain broth into jar, cover and refrigerate up to 1 week. If not using in that time, reheat and rejar.

*To use chicken meat, simmer chicken in broth for 45 minutes. Then remove chicken, skin and set meat aside for another use. Return bones and skin to kettle and continue simmering as directed.

QUICK CHICKEN STOCK

A light stock without the deep flavor of the preceding rich stock.

1 pound chicken bones
1 slice ginger root
1 teaspoon salt
6 cups water

Proceed as with preceding recipe for basic chicken stock, cooking 45 minutes in all.

BASIC FISH STOCK

1 pound fish bones and/or heads
2 green onions, cut up
3 slices ginger root
1 teaspoon salt
8 cups water

Combine ingredients in soup kettle, bring to boil and skim off any scum that rises to surface. Lower heat to simmer, cover and cook 20 minutes. Cool, strain and use within a day. Can be frozen for later use.

BASIC PORK STOCK

2 pounds pork neck or knuckle bones
   with some meat
1 slice ginger root
2 teaspoons salt
8 cups water

Combine ingredients in soup kettle, bring to boil and skim off any scum that rises to surface. Lower heat to simmer, cover and cook slowly 2 hours. Cool, strain into jar, cover and refrigerate up to 1 week. If not using within that time, reheat and rejar.

BASIC BEEF STOCK

Prepare as for Basic Pork Stock, using beef neck or knuckle bones instead of pork.

QUICK PORK STOCK

A lighter stock without the deep flavor of the basic pork stock.

1/2 pound lean pork butt, thinly sliced, or
1 pound pork butt bones with some meat
1 slice ginger root
1 teaspoon salt
6 cups water

Proceed as with basic pork stock, preceding, cooking 45 minutes in all.

CELESTIAL SOUP
Soup for the Gods

Now and then during the course of a feast, even the gods were overwhelmed by the many complex flavors and textures. Their palates needed a bit of clearing before proceeding. This simple soup is often served as a contrasting interlude between heavier Chinese dishes —and to clear the palates of the gods.

6 cups water
2 tablespoons light soy sauce
1 green onion, sliced
1 teaspoon peanut oil
3 drops Oriental sesame oil
1 teaspoon salt

Bring water to boil. In large heated soup bowl, combine soy, onion, peanut and sesame oil and salt. Pour boiling water over and serve immediately.

CHRYSANTHEMUM SOUP

6 cups basic chicken stock
1 cup slivered chicken meat
petals from 6 fresh, large white
   chrysanthemums

Bring stock and chicken to boil, lower heat and simmer 5 minutes. Ladle into individual heated soup bowls and sprinkle with chrysanthemum petals. Serve immediately.

CHRYSANTHEMUM FISH SOUP

1 pound firm white fish fillet
1 teaspoon salt
1 tablespoon rice wine or dry sherry
1 slice ginger root, minced
1 green onion, minced
2 tablespoons peanut oil
6 cups basic chicken stock
4 fresh bean-curd cakes, sliced
1 ounce Virginia ham, slivered
1/2 cup matchstick-cut bamboo shoots
1 egg white, lightly beaten
1 teaspoon Oriental sesame oil
1/4 teaspoon black pepper
petals of 1 large white chrysanthemum
coriander sprigs

Marinate fillet in mixture of salt, wine, ginger root and onion 20 minutes. Heat peanut oil and add stock, bean curd, ham, bamboo shoots and fish with its marinade. Bring to boil, lower heat and cook 10 minutes or until fish is just cooked. Do not overcook. Remove from heat and stir in egg white, sesame oil and pepper. Transfer to heated serving bowl and sprinkle with petals and coriander sprigs.

DUCK LIVER SOUP
Szechwan

1/4 pound fresh duck or chicken livers
6 cups basic chicken stock
1/2 cup sliced bamboo shoots
1/4 cup diced preserved Szechwan cabbage
1 teaspoon light soy sauce
2 teaspoons rice wine or dry sherry
salt and pepper to taste

Blanch livers in 1 cup boiling water 30 seconds. Drain, discard water and thinly slice livers. Heat stock; add livers, bamboo shoots and preserved cabbage. Bring just to boil, remove from heat and add soy, wine and salt and pepper to taste.
Variation with Bean-Thread Noodles When adding livers, add 1 ounce bean-thread noodles, soaked to soften, drained and cut in 4-inch lengths.

SOUPS

WINTER MELON AND SQUAB SOUP IN EARTHEN POT

2 pounds winter melon
1 squab (about 1 pound), whole or halved
1 piece tangerine peel, soaked to soften
4 dried forest mushrooms, soaked to
    soften and halved if large
2 tablespoons lotus seeds
1/2 cup jujubes
1 teaspoon salt
8 cups boiling water

Remove seeds of winter melon and scrub skin clean. Cut into 2-inch chunks and combine with remaining ingredients in heatproof earthen pot. Bring to boil, cover, lower heat and simmer 3 hours.
Variation Half a duck, cut in half, may be substituted for the squab.

DICED WINTER MELON SOUP
Canton

6 cups basic chicken stock
1 piece tangerine peel, soaked to soften
   and minced
6 dried forest mushrooms, soaked to soften
2 pounds winter melon, peeled,
   seeded and cut in 1/2-inch dice
1 cup 1/2-inch dice bamboo shoots
1/4 cup finely slivered Virginia ham

Heat together stock, tangerine peel and mushrooms. Simmer 30 minutes. Raise heat and add winter melon and bamboo shoots. Return to boil, lower heat and simmer 20 minutes. Add ham and serve.

SPARERIB AND MUNG BEAN SPROUT SOUP

1/2 pound pork spareribs, cut in 1-inch pieces
8 cups water
2 slices ginger root
1/2 pound mung bean sprouts
1 ripe tomato, peeled, seeded and diced
salt and pepper to taste

Blanch spareribs 1 minute, rinse, drain and set aside. Bring water and ginger root to boil; add spareribs, lower heat and simmer 45 minutes. Add bean sprouts and tomato, bring back to boil, lower heat and simmer 10 minutes. Season with salt and pepper to taste.

FUZZY MELON SOUP

6 cups basic chicken or pork stock
1 tablespoon dried shrimp (optional)
1 pound fuzzy melon

Bring stock and shrimp to boil, lower heat and simmer 20 minutes. Scrape fuzz off melon and slice melon into pieces 1 inch square and 1/4 inch thick. Add to stock, bring back to boil, lower heat and simmer for 10 minutes.

Variation with Bean Curd Add 2 fresh bean-curd cakes, sliced, during the last 5 minutes of cooking time.

Variation with Bean-Thread Noodles Soak 1 ounce bean-thread noodles in warm water to soften; drain and cut into 3-inch lengths. Add to stock with fuzzy melon. Just before serving season, if desired, with 1/2 teaspoon white pepper and 1/2 teaspoon Oriental sesame oil.

WINE-CHICKEN SOUP

1/2 fryer chicken, cut in bite-size pieces
2 tablespoons Oriental sesame oil
2 slices ginger root
1/2 cup rice wine
6 cups basic chicken stock or water
1 teaspoon each sugar and salt

Heat oil and stir-fry ginger root 1 minute. Add chicken pieces and stir-fry another minute. Add wine, stock or water, sugar and salt. Bring to boil, reduce heat and simmer 20 minutes.

SOUPS

CURRIED BEEF SOUP

1 pound stewing beef, cut into 1-inch cubes
3 slices ginger root
1 tablespoon rice wine or dry sherry
8 cups water
1-1/2 teaspoons salt
1 to 2 teaspoons curry powder, or to taste
2 medium-size potatoes, peeled and cut in
    1-inch chunks

In soup kettle, combine beef, ginger root, wine and water. Bring to boil, skim off any scum that rises to surface, reduce heat, cover and simmer 2 hours or until meat is tender. Add salt, curry powder and potatoes. Bring back to boil, lower heat and cook 10 minutes.

GINGER BEEF BROTH

1/2 pound lean boneless beef chuck, cut
    in 1-inch cubes
1 tablespoon rice wine or dry sherry
4 slices ginger root
1/2 teaspoon salt
4 cups water

In a soup kettle, combine ingredients and bring to boil. Skim off any scum that rises to surface, lower heat, cover and simmer 1-1/2 hours.
Variations Last 10 minutes of cooking add 1/2 pound soybean sprouts or 1/2 pound Napa cabbage, cut into 1-inch pieces.

PORK AND TURNIP SOUP
Szechwan

1 1/2-pound piece pork butt
1 tablespoon salt
1/2 teaspoon Szechwan peppercorns, crushed
6 cups water
1 slice ginger root
2 teaspoons rice wine or dry sherry
1-1/2 pounds Chinese turnips or daikon, cut
    in 1/8-inch thick slices
1/2 cup chopped green onion
1 tablespoon light soy sauce

Sprinkle pork with salt on all sides and refrigerate overnight. Rinse. Heat peppercorns in saucepan until pungent. Add water, bring to boil and add pork, ginger root, wine and turnips or daikon. Bring back to boil, lower heat, cover and simmer 30 minutes. Remove pork, slice thinly and return to soup with green onions and soy sauce. Serve immediately.

MUSTARD GREENS SOUP

1 pound Chinese mustard greens
6 cups basic chicken, pork or beef stock
1 slice ginger root

Coarsely shred mustard green tops and cut stalks into 1-inch diagonal slices. Set aside. Bring stock and ginger to boil, lower heat and simmer 15 minutes. Add greens, bring back to boil, lower heat and simmer 10 minutes.
Variation Substitute spinach, watercress, Napa cabbage or lettuce for the mustard greens.

CHICKEN AND CORN SOUP
Canton

4 cups basic chicken stock
1 whole chicken breast, boned, skinned and
  minced
2 egg whites, stiffly beaten
2 teaspoons light soy sauce
2 cups freshly grated corn kernels
binder of:
  2 tablespoons water
  1 tablespoon cornstarch
salt to taste

Heat stock just to boiling point. Combine
chicken, beaten egg whites and soy; set aside.
Add corn to stock, return just to boil and
simmer 5 minutes. Stir in binder to thicken
slightly. Add chicken mixture and blend well.
Heat through but do not boil. Add salt to
taste and serve immediately.

NAPA CABBAGE OR
ICEBERG LETTUCE SOUP

6 cups basic chicken, pork, beef or
  fish stock
1 head firm Napa cabbage or iceberg lettuce,
  cut in 1-inch square pieces or coarsely
  shredded

Bring stock to boil, add cabbage or lettuce
and bring back to boil. Lower heat and simmer 10 minutes.
Variation If using chicken or pork stock, add
1/4 cup finely slivered Virginia ham during
the last 3 minutes of cooking time.

POACHED EGG SOUP

6 small eggs
1 tablespoon minced coriander
1 tablespoon minced ham
6 cups basic chicken or pork stock
1/4 cup matchstick-cut bamboo shoots
1/4 cup matchstick-cut carrots
4 dried forest mushrooms, soaked to soften
    and cut in matchstick
1 cup fresh green peas
1 tablespoon rice wine or dry sherry
salt to taste

Poach eggs in simmering water until white is set but yolk is still soft, and sprinkle them with coriander and ham. Immediately remove eggs with slotted spoon to cold water. Set aside. Bring stock and vegetables to boil; add wine and salt. With slotted spoon transfer eggs to heated individual serving bowls and pour hot soup over. Serve immediately.

EGG CURD SOUP
Kiangsu

3 eggs
1 tablespoon cornstarch
3 tablespoons lukewarm water
2 tablespoons peanut oil
1/2 cup minced pork butt
2 tablespoons dried shrimp, soaked to soften
    and drained, reserving liquid
1/4 cup matchstick-cut bamboo shoots
4 cups basic chicken or pork stock
2 tomatoes, peeled, seeded and diced
1 cup shredded Napa cabbage or iceberg
    lettuce
salt and white pepper to taste

Beat eggs with cornstarch and water. Place in heatproof bowl and steam over gently boiling water 20 minutes or until firm. Cool slightly, cut into squares and set aside. Heat oil in skillet or wok and stir-fry pork, dried shrimp and bamboo shoots until pork loses its pink color. Add stock and reserved shrimp liquid and bring to boil. Add tomatoes, cabbage and salt and pepper. Bring back just to boil, add egg squares and serve immediately.

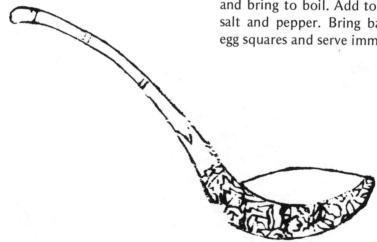

SEAWEED SOUP

6 cups basic chicken, pork or fish stock
1 tablespoon dried shrimp, soaked to soften,
   water reserved
1/4 pound ground pork butt
4 sheets nori (pressed seaweed sheets), or
1 cup dried seaweed, soaked, thoroughly
   rinsed and chopped
2 tablespoons chopped green onion
1/2 teaspoon Oriental sesame oil

Bring stock and dried shrimp with its soaking water to boil. Add pork, lower heat and simmer 10 minutes. Raise heat, add seaweed, bring just to boil, lower heat and simmer 10 minutes. Add green onion and sesame oil.
Variation with Bean Curd Add 2 fresh bean-curd cakes, cut in 1/2-inch dice, during the last 5 minutes of cooking time.

EGG DROP SOUP

6 cups basic chicken or pork stock
2 eggs, beaten
2 tablespoons chopped green onion or chives
1/2 teaspoon Oriental sesame oil (optional)

Bring stock to boil, turn heat to simmer and gradually, in a thin stream, add beaten eggs, stirring constantly. Remove from heat and add onion or chives and sesame oil.
Heavenly Egg Drop Soup When heating stock, add 1/2 cup matchstick-cut bamboo shoots and 4 dried forest mushrooms, soaked to soften and cut in matchstick. Simmer 15 minutes and proceed with egg drop soup recipe.

SHRIMP BALL SOUP
Hangchow

1/2 pound raw shrimp, shelled,
   deveined and minced
2 tablespoons cornstarch
1 tablespoon rice wine or dry sherry
1 teaspoon light soy sauce
1/4 cup peanut oil
6 cups basic chicken stock
4 dried forest mushrooms, soaked to soften
   and thinly sliced
1/2 cup thinly sliced bamboo shoots
2 ounces Virginia ham, slivered
2 leeks, cut in matchstick
binder of:
   2 tablespoons water
   1 tablespoon cornstarch
salt and white pepper to taste

Combine shrimp, cornstarch, wine and soy; blend well. Form into small balls and fry in peanut oil until lightly golden. Remove shrimp balls from pan and set aside. To pan add stock, mushrooms and bamboo shoots. Bring to boil, lower heat and simmer 10 minutes. Add ham, leeks and reserved shrimp balls. Bring just to boil, bind with cornstarch mixture and season with salt and pepper. Serve immediately.
Variation with Scallops Omit shrimp. Cut scallops into quarters if large and coat with cornstarch, wine and soy. Brown and proceed as with shrimp balls.
Variation with Fish Balls Substitute 1/2 pound fish fillet for shrimp.

41

BEAN CURD SOUP

4 cups basic chicken or pork stock
2 fresh bean-curd cakes, cut in 1/2-inch cubes
salt to taste
dash of Oriental sesame oil

Bring stock to boil, add bean curd and return just to boiling point. Remove from heat and season with salt and sesame oil.
Variations When adding bean curd to stock add any one of the following and heat through.
1 cup minced bamboo shoots
1 cup mung bean or soybean sprouts
2 cups shredded Napa cabbage, iceberg
    lettuce, spinach or watercress
1/2 cup diced chicken meat or Virginia ham
1 cup thinly sliced fuzzy melon or cucumber
1 cup fresh green peas
6 to 8 dried forest mushrooms, soaked to
    soften and thinly sliced
2 tablespoons chopped green onion
1 teaspoon chili oil

OYSTER SOUP
Hangchow

1 pint oysters with liquor
1 tablespoon rice wine or dry sherry
1 slice ginger root, minced
1/2 cup minced pork butt
1 tablespoon cornstarch
1 tablespoon light soy sauce
2 tablespoons peanut oil
4 cups water
1 potato, peeled and thinly sliced
1 carrot, thinly sliced
2 leeks, cut in matchstick
salt and white pepper to taste
dash of cayenne pepper (optional)

Drain oysters, reserving liquor, and combine oysters with wine and ginger root. Set aside. Combine pork, cornstarch and soy. Heat peanut oil in wok or skillet and stir-fry pork until it loses its pink color. Add water, oyster liquor, potato and carrot and simmer 15 minutes. Add oysters and leeks. Bring back to boil, season with salt, pepper and cayenne, and serve immediately.

SIZZLING RICE SOUP

A spectacular soup to present at the table, for the hot broth poured over the freshly fried rice crusts makes a delightful sizzling sound. The secret is to have the soup and the rice crusts very hot.

1 tablespoon peanut oil
2 cups hot cooked rice
6 cups chicken stock
1 slice ginger root, minced
6 dried forest mushrooms, soaked to soften and thinly sliced
1/4 cup golden needles, soaked to soften and halved
1/2 cup sliced water chestnuts
3/4 cup matchstick-cut bamboo shoots
1/2 pound Napa cabbage, shredded
1/2 chicken breast, boned and sliced in matchstick
2 fresh bean-curd cakes, cut in 1/2-inch dice
1/2 teaspoon Oriental sesame oil
1/4 teaspoon chili oil
salt to taste
2 tablespoons slivered Virginia ham
peanut oil for deep-frying

Coat baking pan with oil and pat rice firmly into pan to 1/2-inch thickness. Bake in 250° oven until rice kernels are dry. Cut into 1-1/2-inch pieces and set aside. Bring stock, ginger root, mushrooms and golden needles to boil. Lower heat and simmer 20 minutes. Add remaining ingredients except peanut oil and keep hot. Deep-fry the rice crusts in peanut oil until golden, drain and immediately place in heated serving bowl. Pour hot soup over rice crusts and serve *immediately*.

Note Rice crusts may be made ahead; deep-fry when ready to serve.

SZECHWAN CABBAGE AND BEAN-THREAD NOODLE SOUP

4 cups basic chicken or pork stock
1 ounce bean-thread noodles, soaked in hot water to soften, drained and cut into 3-inch lengths
1/3 cup thinly sliced preserved Szechwan cabbage
1/2 cup thinly sliced cucumber
2 tablespoons chopped green onion
1/4 teaspoon black pepper
1/2 teaspoon Oriental sesame oil
1/2 teaspoon light soy sauce
1/2 teaspoon chili oil
salt to taste

Heat stock to boiling, add bean-thread noodles, cabbage and cucumber and bring back to boil. Lower heat and simmer 7 minutes. Add remaining ingredients and serve immediately.

HOT AND SOUR FISH SOUP
Honan

1 carp or other whole white fish (about 2 to 3 pounds)
8 cups water
1/2 cup dried shrimp, soaked to soften, water reserved
1 slice ginger root
1/2 cup sliced bamboo shoots
1 celery rib, sliced
2 tablespoons fish soy
2 tablespoons rice vinegar
1 teaspoon white pepper
1/2 teaspoon Oriental sesame oil
2 or more dried red chili peppers, crushed

Fillet carp and set fillet aside. Combine bones, head and fins with water, bring to boil and simmer, uncovered, 20 minutes. Strain and discard bones. Combine fish stock with shrimp and its soaking water and ginger root. Bring to boil and simmer 10 minutes. Add fillet, bamboo shoots and celery. Cook over medium heat 10 minutes. Season with remaining ingredients and serve.

HOT AND SOUR SOUP
Szechwan

6 cups basic chicken or pork stock
1/3 pound lean pork butt, slivered
6 dried forest mushrooms, soaked to soften
   and cut in matchstick
1/2 cup matchstick-cut bamboo shoots
1/2 cup water chestnuts, sliced
1 teaspoon minced ginger root
1/2 cup cloud ears, soaked to soften
2 fresh bean-curd cakes, thinly sliced
1 tablespoon light soy sauce
1 tablespoon rice wine or dry sherry
2 tablespoons rice vinegar
1/2 teaspoon pepper
salt to taste
1 egg, beaten
2 tablespoons chopped green onion
1/2 teaspoon Oriental sesame oil
1/2 teaspoon chili oil (optional)

Bring stock to boil, add pork, mushrooms, bamboo shoots, water chestnuts, ginger root and cloud ears. Lower heat and simmer 10 minutes. Add bean curd, soy, wine, vinegar and pepper. Bring back just to boil, season to taste with salt and remove from heat. Slowly pour in beaten egg, stirring constantly. Add green onions and sesame and chili oil. Serve immediately.

Variations When bringing stock to boil the first time, add one or more of the following ingredients.
1/4 cup preserved Szechwan cabbage, sliced
1/4 cup golden needles, soaked to soften
1 ounce bean-thread noodles, soaked to
   soften, drained and cut into 3-inch lengths
1/2 pound shredded cabbage, spinach, watercress, lettuce or mustard greens
1 cup fresh green peas

TEA EGGS
Peking

8 eggs
3 tablespoons black tea leaves
1 cinnamon stick
3 whole star anise
1 tablespoon salt
preserved ginger

Boil eggs in water to cover for 10 minutes; drain and let stand in cold water until cool. Crack shells but do not peel. Place eggs, in one layer, in a saucepan with tea leaves, cinnamon stick, star anise and salt. Cover with water and cook over low heat 1 hour. Remove from heat and let cool in tea water. Shell and serve whole or halved with preserved ginger.

PRESERVED ANCIENT EGGS

These are most often called thousand-year eggs, even though the preserving process lasts only 100 days. They may be purchased individually in Oriental markets.

2 cups very strong black tea
1/3 cup salt
2 cups each ashes of pine wood, ashes of
    charcoal and ashes from fireplace
1 cup lime*
12 fresh duck eggs

Combine tea, salt, ashes and lime. Using about 1/2 cup per egg, thickly coat each egg completely with this clay-like mixture. Line a large crock with garden soil and carefully lay coated eggs on top. Cover with more soil and place crock in a cool dark place. Allow to cure for 100 days. To remove coating, scrape eggs and rinse under running water to clean thoroughly. Crack lightly and remove shells. The white of the egg will appear a grayish translucent color and have a gelatinous texture. The yolk, when sliced, will be a grayish-green color.

To serve, cut into wedges and serve with:

Sweet pickled scallions or any sweet pickled vegetable

Sauce of 2 tablespoons each vinegar, soy sauce and rice wine and 1 tablespoon minced ginger root

*Available in garden stores and nurseries

47

SMOKED EGGS
Peking

12 hard-cooked eggs, shelled
1/3 cup light soy sauce
1/2 teaspoon pepper
2 teaspoons sugar
1/3 cup each brown sugar, rice and black
    tea leaves

With thin-tipped sharp knife, make 4 small slits through the white of each egg, barely touching the yolk. (This is done so that the smoke will permeate the eggs.) Combine the soy sauce, pepper and sugar, and marinate eggs in this mixture at least 3 hours, turning once. Mix together brown sugar, tea leaves and rice, and spread evenly on bottom of a heavy iron skillet lined with foil. Place a rack on top of tea-rice mixture and arrange eggs on rack. Place skillet on low heat until smoke appears. Let smoke permeate eggs 3 to 5 minutes and then turn them over to smoke the other side for 3 minutes. Immediately return eggs to marinade and let cool. Discard the tea-rice mixture. Serve eggs cut in half.

SALTED EGGS

1-1/2 cups rock salt
4 cups water
12 fresh eggs, preferably duck eggs

Bring water and rock salt to a boil; cool. Place eggs in a crock or glass jar. Pour salt-water mixture over eggs to cover. Cover crock and let stand in a cool place (not refrigerator) for 3 weeks. Remove eggs from salt bath and store them in the refrigerator if not ready to use immediately. Yolks should be a bright yellow-orange color and quite firm. The white should be slightly cloudy and still runny. Eggs without a firm yolk should be discarded. To hard cook, cover with fresh cold water and simmer 20 minutes. Shell and quarter. Serve with hot rice or congee.

Note Salted duck eggs may be purchased in mud-pack form or in brine in Oriental markets. If in mud pack, scrape off mud, wash well and proceed with recipe.

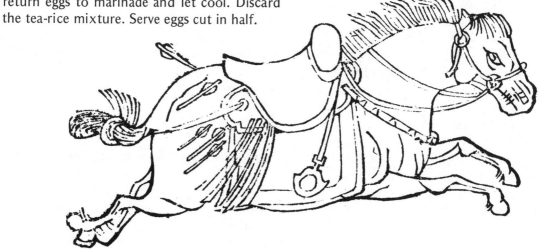

STEAMED SALTED DUCK EGG WITH PORK

2 salted duck eggs, uncooked (preceding)
1 fresh egg, beaten
1/2 cup water
1/2 pound ground pork butt
2 tablespoons cornstarch
1/2 teaspoon Oriental sesame oil
2 tablespoons finely minced green onion

Separate yolks and whites of duck eggs. Set yolks aside and combine whites with remaining ingredients. Pat mixture evenly in a shallow heatproof dish, at least 1/2 inch from rim of dish. Cut yolks into quarters and arrange on top of pork mixture. Steam over boiling water 30 minutes. Serve hot.

STEAMED ANCIENT EGG DIAMONDS

3 fresh eggs
1/4 cup hot water
1 teaspoon peanut oil
1 preserved ancient egg, cleaned, shelled and diced (page 47)
1 salted duck egg, hard cooked, shelled and diced (page 48)
coriander sprigs
preserved ginger and slivered green onion

Beat fresh eggs and gradually add hot water and oil. Stir in diced preserved egg and salted duck egg. Pour into a shallow, oiled heatproof dish and steam over gently boiling water 15 minutes or until eggs are set. Let cool in dish and cut into small diamonds. Garnish with coriander. Serve with preserved ginger and slivered green onion.
Note If serving hot for main dish, increase water to 1 cup.

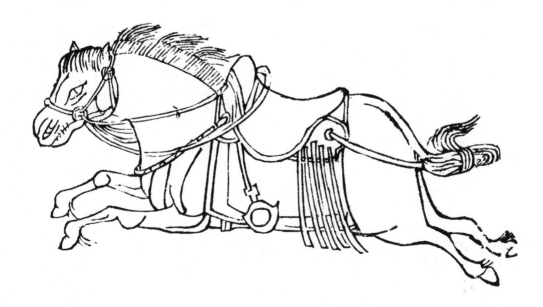

EGGS

EGG SLIVERS

4 eggs, beaten
2 tablespoons water
1/4 teaspoon salt
1 tablespoon peanut oil

Combine eggs, water and salt. Heat a 12-inch skillet over medium heat, add half the peanut oil and pour in half the egg mixture, tilting pan to coat surface. Cook until eggs are just set, moist but not runny. Bottom should be slightly golden. Turn out onto board and repeat with remaining oil and egg mixture. Let cool, roll and slice into slivers.

GOLDEN COIN EGGS
Hunan

6 hard-cooked eggs, shelled and sliced into
   1/2-inch crosswise slices
2 tablespoons cornstarch
3 tablespoons peanut oil
1 hot green chili pepper, minced
1 teaspoon minced ginger root
2 tablespoons minced green onion
2 tablespoons light soy sauce
1 tablespoon rice vinegar
1 tablespoon rice wine or dry sherry
1 teaspoon sugar
1/2 teaspoon Oriental sesame oil
shredded iceberg lettuce

Coat egg slices lightly with cornstarch and brown lightly in peanut oil. Combine remaining ingredients, except lettuce, add to egg slices and mix gently. Heat through and pour over bed of shredded lettuce.

EGG ROLLS
Peking

3/4 pound ground white fish or shrimp
2 teaspoons rice wine or dry sherry
1 teaspoon light soy sauce
1 teaspoon fish soy
1 thin slice ginger root, minced
1 tablespoon cornstarch
3 tablespoons chopped green onion
3 eggs, beaten with
dash of sugar
paste of 2 tablespoons each flour and water
vegetable oil for deep-frying

Combine fish, wine, soy sauce, fish soy, ginger root, cornstarch and green onion. Set aside. Lightly oil a heavy skillet or omelet pan and heat. Pour in one-sixth of the egg mixture, tilting pan to cover bottom. Let set and remove to plate. Repeat with remaining egg, making 6 egg pancakes in all. Divide fish mixture into 6 portions and spread evenly on each pancake. Roll up, sealing edges with paste. Deep-fry, seam side down, 3 minutes or until golden and cooked through. Drain.
Variations with Meat or Poultry Omit fish soy and substitute ground chicken, beef or lamb for the fish, adding 1/2 teaspoon Oriental sesame oil and a pinch of five-spice powder.

STEAMED EGG CUSTARD

4 eggs
1 teaspoon peanut oil
1-1/2 cups hot water
1/2 teaspoon salt
1/4 teaspoon white pepper
1/4 cup chopped green onion
1 tablespoon soy sauce or oyster sauce
dash of Oriental sesame oil

In heatproof bowl, beat eggs and peanut oil. Gradually beat in hot water, blending well, and add salt and pepper. Sprinkle onions on top and steam above gently boiling water 15 minutes or until eggs are just set. The use of hot liquid instead of cold results in a smooth, custard texture. Just before serving, drizzle with soy or oyster sauce and sesame oil.

Variations Just before steaming, add any one of the following.

1/2 cup minced raw beef, chicken, fish, shrimp, oysters, or any minced leftover meat
1 Chinese sausage, chopped
1 tablespoon dried shrimp, soaked to soften
1/4 cup minced raw ham
1 tablespoon chopped coriander
3 to 4 dried forest mushrooms, soaked to soften and chopped
1/2 cup chopped water chestnuts and/or bamboo shoots
1 cup chopped spinach or peeled, diced tomatoes
1 cup diced fresh bean curd (reduce liquid to 1 cup)

EGGS

BRAINS FOO YUNG

1/2 pound brains, any kind
1 slice ginger root
4 eggs, beaten
1 cup mung bean sprouts, blanched
   1 minute and drained
2 tablespoons chopped green onion or
   Chinese chives
1 tablespoon chopped coriander
1 tablespoon cornstarch
1 teaspoon rice wine or dry sherry
1 teaspoon light soy sauce
1/4 teaspoon Oriental sesame oil
3 tablespoons peanut oil

Soak brains in cold water to cover 10 minutes. Remove outer membrane and parboil with the ginger root in water to cover 5 minutes or until firm. Let cool in water, drain, dice and combine with remaining ingredients except peanut oil. Heat oil in a skillet and drop in batter by tablespoonfuls, making 3-inch cakes. When set, turn to cook other side. Repeat until all cakes have been cooked.

CHICKEN AND HAM FOO YUNG
Hangchow

1/2 raw chicken breast, skinned, boned
   and slivered
1 teaspoon cornstarch
1 teaspoon light soy sauce
1 teaspoon rice wine or dry sherry
peanut oil for cooking
2 ounces Virginia ham, slivered
3 to 4 dried forest mushrooms, soaked
   to soften and cut in matchstick
1/2 cup matchstick-cut bamboo shoots
1/2 cup fresh green peas
6 egg whites, stiffly beaten with
1/2 teaspoon salt

Combine chicken, cornstarch, soy and wine. Let stand 30 minutes to blend flavors. Heat 2 tablespoons oil in heavy skillet or wok and stir-fry chicken mixture 2 minutes. Remove chicken mixture from pan and set aside to cool. Heat 2 more tablespoons oil and stir-fry ham, mushrooms, bamboo shoots and peas 3 minutes or until peas are just tender, adding a little water if needed. Remove from pan and set aside. Blend cooled chicken into beaten egg whites. Heat 2 tablespoons oil in skillet. Add egg white mixture, tilting pan to cover entire bottom. Do not stir. When almost set, but not dry, cover with ham and vegetable mixture. Cover and let steam rise to surface, about 1 minute. Invert onto heated platter and serve immediately.

FISH EGG FOO YUNG
Canton

6 eggs, beaten with
4 half egg shells of water
1/2 pound ground fish
1 tablespoon light soy sauce
dash of salt
2 tablespoons cornstarch
1/2 teaspoon Oriental sesame oil
1/2 cup each chopped water chestnuts
   and celery
2 tablespoons chopped green onion
2 cups mung bean sprouts, blanched
   1 minute and drained
1/3 cup peanut oil
1 cup chicken stock
1 tablespoon oyster sauce or soy sauce
binder of:
   2 tablespoons water
   1 tablespoon cornstarch
1/4 cup chopped green onion

Beat the eggs with the water and combine with fish, soy, salt, cornstarch, sesame oil, water chestnuts, celery, onion and bean sprouts. Heat 2 tablespoons oil in skillet and drop batter by tablespoonfuls into hot oil, making 3-inch cakes. When set, turn to cook other side. Remove to heated serving platter and keep warm. Repeat until all cakes have been cooked, adding more oil as needed. Combine stock and oyster or soy sauce in skillet. Bring to boil and bind with cornstarch mixture. Pour over egg foo yung and serve immediately garnished with green onion.
Variation Substitute 1/2 pound shrimp, minced, or 1/2 pound flaked crab meat for ground fish.

EGG MEATBALLS ON SPINACH

1/2 pound ground pork butt
1/4 pound raw shrimp, minced
3 dried forest mushrooms, soaked to
    soften and minced
1 teaspoon salt
1/2 teaspoon sugar
1 teaspoon Oriental sesame oil
1 tablespoon each water and cornstarch.
egg slivers (page 50)
1 bunch fresh spinach
1 tablespoon peanut oil
1 tablespoon rice wine or dry sherry
1 cup chicken or pork stock
binder of:
    2 teaspoons cornstarch
    2 teaspoons water

Combine pork, shrimp, mushrooms, salt, sugar, sesame oil, water and cornstarch. Shape into walnut-size balls. Coat meatballs with egg slivers, pressing in firmly. Place in shallow heatproof dish and steam over boiling water 12 minutes. Blanch spinach 30 seconds and drain well. Place spinach leaves on heated platter and arrange meatballs on top. Keep warm. Bring peanut oil, wine and stock to boil. Bind with cornstarch mixture and pour over meatballs and spinach.

STIRRED EGGS WITH BEAN-THREAD NOODLES
Canton

1 ounce bean-thread noodles
1/4 pound lean ground pork butt
1 teaspoon light soy sauce
1 teaspoon cornstarch
2 teaspoons peanut oil
1/2 teaspoon salt
1/4 teaspoon white pepper
3 tablespoons peanut oil
2 ounces smoked ham, cut in matchstick
1 celery rib, chopped
1/4 cup chopped green onion or Chinese
    chives
2 tablespoons chopped coriander
6 eggs, beaten
oyster sauce, soy sauce and/or chili oil

Soak bean-thread noodles in warm water to soften and parboil 1 minute. Drain, cut into 4-inch lengths and set aside. Combine pork, soy sauce, cornstarch, 2 teaspoons peanut oil, salt and pepper. Heat 2 tablespoons peanut oil in heavy skillet or wok and stir-fry pork mixture and ham 1 minute. Add celery, onion and coriander and stir-fry another minute. Add reserved noodles, cover skillet and cook 2 minutes, adding a little water if noodles stick. Pour in beaten eggs and scramble over low heat until eggs begin to set but are still moist. Turn out on heated platter and serve with oyster sauce, soy sauce and/or chili oil.

PEKING STIRRED EGG YOLKS

6 large egg yolks, beaten
1/2 cup minced water chestnuts
1-1/2 cups basic chicken stock
1 teaspoon rice wine or dry sherry
3 tablespoons peanut oil
1/4 cup minced cooked Virginia ham

Combine yolks, water chestnuts, stock and wine. Heat oil in heavy skillet over medium heat and pour in egg mixture. Cook, stirring gently and constantly in a circular motion along bottom and edge until mixture turns to a soft, smooth, moist consistency. Garnish with minced ham and serve immediately.

STIRRED EGGS AND PEAS

1 tablespoon peanut oil
1/2 cup minced raw ham, or
2 slices bacon, cut in 1/2-inch dice
1 cup fresh green peas
1/2 cup water
6 eggs, beaten
1 tablespoon rice wine or dry sherry
1/4 cup chopped green onion
oyster sauce (optional)

Heat peanut oil in a wok or skillet and stir-fry ham or bacon 1 minute. Add peas, stir well, and blend in water. Simmer, covered, until peas are just tender. Combine eggs, wine and green onion. Increase heat to medium, pour egg mixture over peas and cook, stirring occasionally, until eggs are set and still moist. Turn out onto heated platter and serve with oyster sauce, if desired.

STIRRED EGGS AND CHINESE CHIVES

4 eggs, beaten
1/2 cup water
1 teaspoon peanut oil
1/2 teaspoon Oriental sesame oil
1 cup chopped Chinese chives
1/4 teaspoon white pepper
1 tablespoon peanut oil
oyster sauce or soy sauce

Combine eggs, water, 1 teaspoon peanut oil, sesame oil, chives and pepper. Heat 1 tablespoon peanut oil in skillet over medium heat. Pour in egg mixture. When beginning to set on the bottom, stir as you would scrambled eggs and continue cooking until just set and moist. Turn out onto hot platter and serve with either oyster sauce or soy sauce.

55

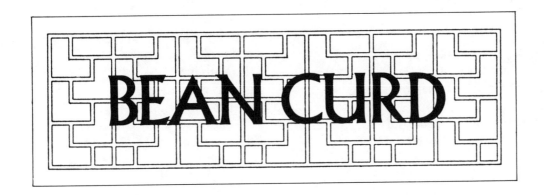

BEAN CURD

THE SOYBEAN

Known as the "cow of China," the versatile, protein-loaded soybean appears in many forms throughout Chinese cooking. It provides oil; its curds can be formed into cakes, fermented like cheese or dried in sheets. As a fresh vegetable its sprouts add a unique crunchy texture and mild flavor to many a dish. And Chinese cooks would be lost without the ubiquitous, tasty, fermented soy sauce with all its different flavors and colors.

PRESSED BEAN CURD

Cakes of fresh bean curd are too filled with water for some purposes. A home method of squeezing out the excess moisture can easily be improvised. Probably the simplest method is to put the bean cakes on a sheet of wax paper spread over a smooth board or counter top. Cover with another sheet of wax paper and place a smooth board on top. Then add weights or books; let stand several hours.

BEAN CURD SALAD
Szechwan

4 fresh bean-curd cakes
2 tablespoons small dried shrimp, soaked
    to soften (optional)
1 cucumber, peeled if skin is tough, seeded
    and cut in matchstick
2 or more dried red chili peppers, crushed
2 tablespoons rice vinegar
1 teaspoon Oriental sesame oil
1 tablespoon fish soy
3 tablespoons peanut oil

Parboil bean curd 1 minute and drain well. Let cool and slice thinly or cut into 1/2-inch dice. Combine with remaining ingredients. Chill before serving.
Variation Add 1/2 cup cooked shredded chicken, ham or shrimp.

BEAN CURD

COLD BEAN-CURD APPETIZER
Hunan

4 fresh bean-curd cakes, cut into 1-inch cubes
1/4 cup light soy sauce
1/2 teaspoon Oriental sesame oil
1 teaspoon sugar
1 teaspoon minced ginger root
1 tablespoon minced green onion
1/2 teaspoon chili oil
salt and white pepper to taste

Combine ingredients and chill. Serve as a refreshing light appetizer.

BEAN CURD AND PEANUT SALAD
Shanghai

4 pressed bean-curd cakes (page 57), cut
   in 1/2-inch dice
1/2 cup shelled roasted peanuts, coarsely
   chopped
1/2 cup diced celery
1/2 cup diced bell pepper
2 tablespoons light soy sauce
1 teaspoon Oriental sesame oil
1 teaspoon sugar
salt and white pepper to taste

Combine ingredients and blend well. Serve at room temperature.
Variations Add 1 cup blanched mung bean sprouts or 1/2 cup each blanched peas and diced carrots.

DEEP-FRIED BEAN CURD

4 fresh bean-curd cakes, cut in 1-inch cubes
peanut oil for deep-frying
salt (optional)
dipping sauce of:
   1 teaspoon chili oil
   1 teaspoon Oriental sesame oil
   1 tablespoon light soy sauce
   1 tablespoon sesame-seed paste or
      peanut butter
   1 tablespoon peanut oil

Pat bean-curd cubes with paper toweling to remove excess moisture. Heat oil and fry cubes, without crowding, until puffed and golden. Drain on paper toweling and sprinkle with salt if desired. Serve with sauce.
Note Deep-fried bean curd may be added to any vegetable or meat stir-fry dish, adding the last minute to retain crispness.

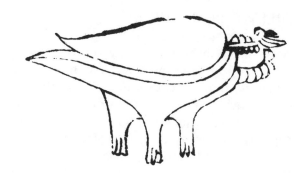

STIR-FRIED BEAN CURD

3 tablespoons peanut oil
2 green onions, cut in 1-inch lengths
4 fresh bean-curd cakes, cut in 1-inch cubes
2 tablespoons soy sauce
salt and pepper to taste

Heat oil in wok or skillet and stir-fry onions 1 minute. Carefully add bean-curd cubes and gently stir-fry until lightly golden, tilting or shaking pan and using a flat spatula to turn once. Drizzle soy sauce over and sprinkle with salt and pepper. Serve immediately.

Variations

Substitute 1 tablespoon oyster sauce or brown
    bean sauce for 1 tablespoon of the soy sauce.
Add 1 cup cooked, sliced Chinese sausage or
    Chinese barbecued pork to the pan with
    the green onions.
Add 1/2 cup raw shrimp with the green onions.
Mince the onions instead of cutting in lengths,
    and stir-fry with 1/2 pound ground pork
    butt and 1 dried red chili pepper, crushed.
Before stir-frying the onions, stir-fry 1 cup
    fresh green peas and 4 dried forest
    mushrooms, soaked to soften and diced,
    for 2 minutes.

MA PO BEAN CURD
Szechwan

3 tablespoons peanut oil
1/4 pound minced pork butt
2 garlic cloves, minced
2 tablespoons minced green onion
1 teaspoon minced ginger root
4 fresh bean-curd cakes, cut in
    1/2-inch dice
1 tablespoon each light soy sauce and hot
    bean paste
1/2 cup basic chicken stock or water
1/2 teaspoon salt
binder of:
    1 tablespoon water
    1 teaspoon cornstarch
1 teaspoon chili oil

Heat 1 tablespoon of the peanut oil in a wok or skillet and stir-fry pork 3 minutes or until cooked through. Remove pork and set aside. Add remaining peanut oil to pan and stir-fry garlic, green onion and ginger root for 1 minute. Add bean curd, soy sauce, bean paste, stock, salt and reserved pork. Cover and cook 3 minutes. Bind with cornstarch mixture and transfer to serving dish. Sprinkle with chili oil.

BEAN CURD

STUFFED BEAN CURD
Canton

4 pressed bean-curd cakes (page 57)
1/2 pound ground white fish
2 tablespoons chopped green onion
1 tablespoon chopped coriander
1 piece tangerine peel, soaked to soften and
  minced
1/2 cup minced water chestnuts
1/2 teaspoon salt
1 teaspoon fish soy
2 tablespoons water
2 teaspoons cornstarch
1/3 cup peanut oil
1-1/2 cups basic fish, chicken or pork stock
1 tablespoon oyster sauce
binder of:
   3 tablespoons water
   1 tablespoon cornstarch
coriander sprigs
matchstick-cut green onions

Cut each piece of pressed bean curd into 2 triangles. Then, make a slit, without cutting through, in long edge of each triangle to form a pocket. Combine fish, green onion, coriander, tangerine peel, water chestnuts, salt, fish soy, water and cornstarch. Stuff a heaping teaspoon of this mixture into pocket of each bean-curd triangle. Heat oil and fry triangles, slit side down, 2 minutes or until golden, shaking pan lightly to prevent sticking. Turn to brown other side. Add stock, cover and simmer 3 minutes. Carefully remove triangles with spatula. Add oyster sauce and binder to skillet and cook and stir until thickened. Pour over triangles and garnish with coriander and green onions.

Note If desired, bean-curd cakes may be cut into halves instead of triangles. They may also be steamed: After stuffing, arrange in shallow heatproof dish, drizzle with a little oyster or soy sauce and steam over gently boiling water 30 minutes.

BEAN CURD IN EARTHEN POT

4 fresh bean-curd cakes, cut in quarters
6 dried forest mushrooms, soaked to soften
    and quartered
1/2 cup sliced bamboo shoots
2 leeks, cut in 1-inch lengths
5 cups basic chicken stock
1 tablespoon rice wine or dry sherry
1/4 pound pork butt, thinly sliced
1/4 pound raw shrimp, shelled and deveined
salt to taste

Place bean curd, mushrooms, bamboo shoots
and leeks in heatproof earthen pot. Pour in
stock and wine and top with pork. Bring to
gentle boil, cover, lower heat and simmer 40
minutes. Add shrimp and cook another 3 minutes. Season to taste with salt.

BEAN CURD CASSEROLE

4 fresh bean-curd cakes
1 whole chicken breast, cut in bite-size pieces
2 tablespoons dried shrimp, soaked to soften
2 green onions, cut in 1-inch lengths
1 teaspoon minced ginger root
4 dried forest mushrooms, soaked to soften
    and sliced
1/2 cup sliced bamboo shoots
6 cups basic chicken stock, heated
1/2 cup slivered Virginia ham
1/2 pound spinach, trimmed

Line heatproof earthen pot with bean curd
cakes. Add chicken, shrimp, onions, ginger
root, mushrooms and bamboo shoots. Pour in
stock, cover and cook over medium heat 30
minutes; add ham and spinach last 5 minutes.

BEAN CURD WITH MEAT AND VEGETABLES
Shanghai

3 tablespoons peanut oil
1/4 cup diced ham
1 cup diced chicken or pork
3 or 4 dried forest mushrooms, soaked to
    soften and diced
1 cup diced bamboo shoots
1 cup basic chicken stock
1 tablespoon light soy sauce
1 teaspoon rice wine or dry sherry
1 cup fresh green peas
4 pressed bean-curd cakes (page 57),
    cut in 1/2-inch dice
1/2 cup flaked crab meat (optional)
binder of:
    1 tablespoon water
    1 tablespoon cornstarch
salt and pepper to taste

Heat oil in wok or skillet and stir-fry ham,
chicken or pork, mushrooms and bamboo
shoots 2 minutes. Add stock, soy and wine.
Bring to boil and add peas and bean curd.
Cook another minute and add crab meat.
Bind with cornstarch mixture and season to
taste with salt and pepper.

BEAN CURD WITH EGG YOLKS AND MIXED MEATS
Peking

4 fresh bean-curd cakes
4 egg yolks, beaten
1/2 cup basic chicken stock
1 tablespoon cornstarch
5 tablespoons peanut oil
1 tablespoon dried shrimp, soaked to
   soften and minced
1/4 cup each minced raw ham and raw
   pork butt
2 tablespoons brown bean sauce
1 teaspoon light soy sauce
1/2 teaspoon Oriental sesame oil
2 tablespoons chopped green onion

Crumble bean-curd cakes and combine with egg yolks, stock and cornstarch; set aside. Heat 2 tablespoons of the peanut oil in wok or skillet and stir-fry the shrimp, ham and pork with the brown bean sauce, soy and sesame oil for 2 minutes, or until cooked through. Remove and set aside. Add remaining oil to skillet, heat and add bean curd and egg mixture. Cook over medium heat until center of mixture starts to boil. Pour into deep, heated serving bowl and sprinkle with reserved meat mixture and chopped green onions. Serve immediately.

MOCK CHICKEN

3/4 cup basic chicken stock
2 tablespoons light soy sauce
1 tablespoon sugar
1 tablespoon Oriental sesame oil
1 teaspoon salt
8 dried bean-curd sheets, soaked to soften
peanut oil for deep-frying

Bring stock, soy, sugar, sesame oil and salt to boil. Cool. Fold bean-curd sheets into oblongs (approximately 4 by 8 inches) and stack the sheets on top of each other, spooning the stock mixture between each layer. Roll stacked sheets into oblong loaf, wrap in cheesecloth and steam on rack over boiling water 20 minutes. Remove cheesecloth and fry loaf in deep oil until golden. Drain and cut into 1/2-inch diagonal slices.

STEAMED BEAN CURD WITH PORK
Peking

4 fresh bean-curd cakes
1/2 pound ground pork butt
1 teaspoon chopped ginger root
1 green onion, chopped
1 tablespoon light soy sauce
2 teaspoons brown bean sauce
1 tablespoon rice wine or dry sherry
1 teaspoon Oriental sesame oil
1/2 teaspoon each salt and sugar

Parboil bean curd 1 minute and drain. Arrange in shallow heatproof dish. Combine remaining ingredients and spread on top of bean-curd cakes. Steam over gently boiling water 25 minutes.

FERMENTED BLACK BEANS
WITH BEAN-CURD CAKES
Buddhist

4 fresh bean-curd cakes, cut in 1/2-inch dice
peanut oil for deep-frying
1 tablespoon Oriental sesame oil
2 tablespoons fermented black beans,
    rinsed and mashed
1 tablespoon minced ginger root
1 tablespoon light soy sauce
1/2 cup water
1 tablespoon sugar

Deep-fry bean-curd cubes in peanut oil over
moderate heat until lightly golden. Drain with
slotted spoon and set aside. Heat sesame oil
in a wok or skillet and stir-fry fermented
black beans 2 minutes. Add remaining ingredients, bring to boil and add reserved fried
bean-curd cubes. Cover and cook 10 minutes
over medium heat until most of liquid has
boiled away. Serve immediately.

STEAMED BEAN-CURD ROLLS

4 dried bean-curd sheets
1/4 pound shelled raw shrimp, minced
1/4 pound ground lean pork butt
1 green onion, minced
1 slice ginger root, minced
1/2 teaspoon salt
3 dried forest mushrooms, soaked to soften
    and cut in matchstick
1/2 cup matchstick-cut bamboo shoots
2 teaspoons light soy sauce
binder of:
    2 teaspoons water
    1 teaspoon cornstarch
1/2 teaspoon Oriental sesame oil

Soak bean-curd sheets until pliable; drain and
place each sheet flat on board. Combine
remaining ingredients except binder and
sesame oil and divide evenly on the 4 bean-
curd sheets. Roll over once, fold in edges and
roll like jelly roll. Place in shallow heatproof
dish and steam over boiling water 25 minutes.
Cut into 1-inch pieces and set aside. Pour
accumulated liquid (about 1/2 cup) into a
saucepan. Bind with cornstarch mixture and
add sesame oil. Pour over rolls and serve immediately.

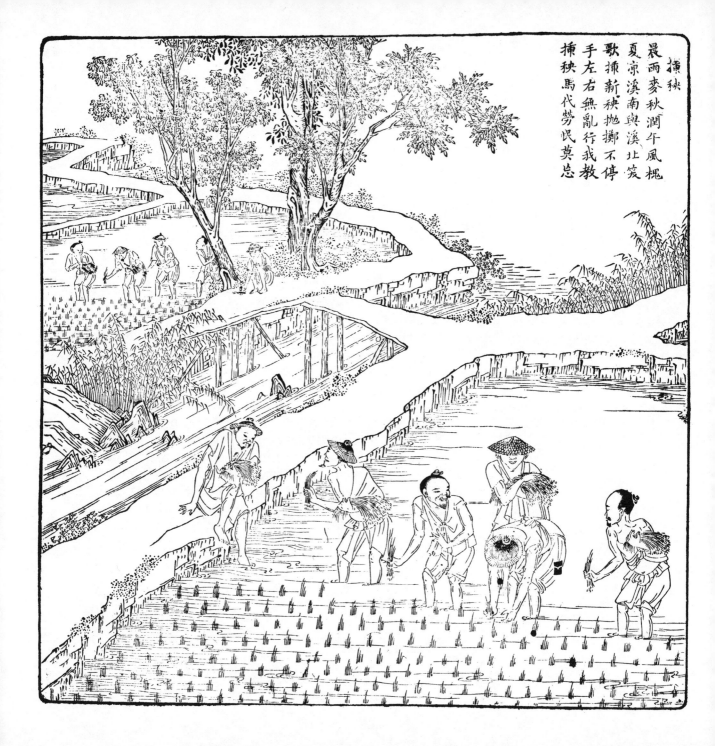

插秧

晨雨麥秋潤午風
夏涼溪南與溪北
歌插新秧抛擲不傳
手左右無亂行我教
插秧馬代勞民莫怠

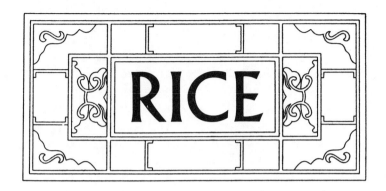

RICE

STEAMED RICE

The Chinese most often use long-grain white rice to make the steamed rice served with their meals. To make a perfect pot of steamed rice, always cook at least 1 cup of raw rice, and plan on about 1/3 cup of raw rice per person. Select a saucepan with a tight-fitting lid. The pan should be large enough to allow for the rice to expand during cooking, at least twice the volume of rice being cooked, but not so large that the rice becomes too much of a crust. Measure the amount of rice needed into the saucepan and thoroughly wash the rice by holding the pan under cold running water and moving the kernels about with your fingers. This should be done about 3 or 4 times until the water runs clear. Washing rids the kernels of excess starch. Once the rice is thoroughly rinsed, add water to cover by approximately 3/4 inch (about 1-1/4 cups of water for each cup of rice). If possible, allow the rice to stand at this point for about 30 minutes before cooking it. This soaking will shorten the cooking time and the kernels will

cook more evenly and thoroughly. To cook the rice, place the saucepan over high heat, uncovered, until the water and bubbles disappear from the surface. Cover the pot and reduce the heat to a low simmer and cook for 15 minutes. When the rice is cooked, fluff up the kernels with chopsticks and serve. Rice cooked by this method will form a crust on the bottom. The rice crust may be eaten as is or spread with fermented bean cake, used for sizzling rice soup, or boiling water may be added to the pot to make rice tea.

How to Save a Pot of Burnt Rice If the rice should scorch while it is cooking, the pot of rice may still be rescued. Simply place a dampened cloth or a slice of bread and 1 or 2 tablespoons of water over the surface of the rice, cover, lower the heat to a simmer and cook until rice is tender. The cloth or bread will absorb the burnt smell.

Steamed Glutinous Rice Glutinous rice may be prepared in the same manner as steamed long-grain rice by increasing the soaking period to 4 hours and the cooking time to 35 minutes.

R I C E

REHEATING RICE

How to Reheat Rice Cooked rice may be reheated in several ways. To reheat by simmering, place the rice in a saucepan with a tight-fitting lid. Then for each cup of rice, sprinkle 1 tablespoon of water over the surface of the rice, cover and simmer over low heat until the rice is hot. To reheat by steaming, place the rice in a heatproof bowl, sieve or colander and place this with about 2 inches of water in a large pot. Cover and steam over medium heat for 10 minutes or until heated through. To reheat in the oven, place rice in heatproof dish or pan and sprinkle 1 tablespoon of water for each cup of rice over the surface. Place, covered, in a preheated 400° oven for 20 minutes.

PORK FRIED RICE

3 tablespoons peanut oil
4 cups cooked rice
2 tablespoons soy sauce or oyster sauce
1 teaspoon sugar
salt and pepper to taste
1 cup slivered Chinese barbecued pork
1 cup fresh green peas, blanched
    30 seconds and drained
egg slivers (page 50)
1/2 cup chopped green onions
chopped coriander (optional)
1/2 teaspoon Oriental sesame oil

Heat peanut oil in a wok or skillet until it sizzles. Add rice, soy or oyster sauce, sugar, salt and pepper, stirring constantly to blend well and prevent rice from sticking. When thoroughly heated, add pork, peas and egg slivers and heat through. Toss in the green onions, coriander and sesame oil and serve.
Variations Any of the following cooked (or stir-fried) ingredients may be added.
Bamboo shoots, bean sprouts, dried forest mushrooms, soaked to soften, celery, water chestnuts
Chicken, duck, turkey, beef, ham, lamb, Chinese sausage, shrimp

CONGEE
(Jook)

Although congee is actually a soup, it is never served as a soup course. The Chinese often serve it for breakfast or as a late-night snack.

1 cup long-grain rice
3 quarts stock
2 tablespoons minced Chinese
    preserved turnip
1 slice ginger root, minced
1 piece tangerine peel, soaked to soften
    and minced
salt
garnish of:
    chopped green onion
    chopped coriander
    slivered preserved ginger
    sliced tea melon

Combine rice, stock, preserved turnip, ginger and tangerine peel in a large soup pot and bring to boil. Lower heat and simmer, uncovered, approximately 1-1/2 hours or until the rice is thoroughly broken up. Stir occasionally to prevent soup from sticking and add boiling water if necessary. When done, soup should be thick and creamy. Add salt to taste and garnish with any or all of the suggested garnishes.
Variations Just before serving, add cooked chicken, pork, ham or beef. Or with rice add diced forest mushrooms, soaked to soften, or dried shrimp.

GLUTINOUS RICE WITH
HAM AND DRIED SHRIMP

Glutinous rice is a sticky rice high in the B vitamins. Many Chinese eat it in the winter time because its high protein content keeps them warm.

3 cups glutinous rice, washed and soaked
    2 hours, then drained
3 cups water
1/2 cup slivered ham
1/4 cup dried shrimp, soaked to soften
4 dried forest mushrooms, soaked to soften
    and cut in matchstick
1 piece Chinese preserved turnip, rinsed and
    finely minced
1 teaspoon Oriental sesame oil

Place rice in a heatproof earthen pot. Add water and bring to boil. Lower heat to medium and cook, uncovered, until all water is absorbed. Combine remaining ingredients and place on top of rice. Cover and cook at lowest heat 20 minutes. Let stand 10 minutes before serving.

ONE-POT RICE DISHES

Popular with the Chinese, one-pot rice dishes are simple to prepare for any meal of the day. The rice absorbs the delicious flavors of the meats and seasoning as they cook on its surface. Glutinous rice (or half regular rice and half glutinous rice) may also be used for these recipes.

BEEF AND RICE

2 cups raw rice
1 pound lean ground beef
2 tablespoons soy sauce or oyster sauce
1 or 2 slices ginger root, minced
2 tablespoons chopped green onion

Prepare and cook rice according to directions for steamed rice on page 65. Combine remaining ingredients. When all of the water and bubbles have disappeared from the surface, crumble the meat mixture on top. Turn heat down to low simmer, cover with a tight-fitting lid and cook 15 to 20 minutes.

CHINESE SAUSAGE AND RICE

2 cups raw rice
4 Chinese sausages
soy sauce

Prepare and cook rice according to directions for steamed rice on page 65. When all of the water and bubbles have disappeared from the surface, place the whole Chinese sausages on top. Turn heat down to a low simmer, cover with a tight-fitting lid and cook 15 to 20 minutes. When the sausages and rice are cooked, slice the sausages and serve them with the rice drizzled with soy sauce.

CHICKEN, MUSHROOM, BAMBOO SHOOTS AND RICE

2 cups raw rice
1 cup slivered raw chicken meat
1/2 cup matchstick-cut bamboo shoots
4 forest mushrooms, soaked to soften
   and slivered
2 tablespoons chopped green onion
1 tablespoon soy sauce
1 teaspoon rice wine or dry sherry
1 teaspoon peanut oil

Prepare and cook rice according to directions for steamed rice on page 65. Combine all remaining ingredients. When all of the water and bubbles have disappeared from the surface, place the chicken mixture on top of the rice. Turn heat down to low simmer, cover with a tight-fitting lid and cook 15 to 20 minutes.

HAM, PEAS, EGGS AND RICE

2 cups raw rice
1 cup slivered ham
1 cup fresh green peas
egg yolks
soy sauce or oyster sauce

Prepare and cook rice according to directions for steamed rice on page 65. When all of the water and bubbles have disappeared from the surface, place the ham and peas on top of the rice. Turn heat down to low simmer, cover with a tight-fitting lid and cook 15 to 20 minutes. Place 1 egg yolk in the bottom of each bowl. Spoon rice and ham mixture on top and serve. The steam from the rice will just set the egg. Serve with soy or oyster sauce.

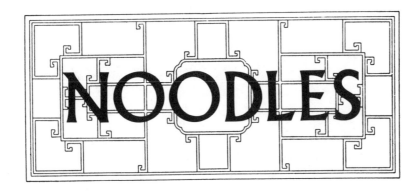

NOODLES

EGG NOODLE DOUGH

3 or more cups unbleached flour
4 eggs, lightly beaten
cornstarch for dusting

Combine flour with eggs and form into ball. Knead 10 minutes, form into ball again and cover with dampened tea towel. Let rest 20 minutes. Knead again on floured board and roll out as thinly as possible in several batches. Keep dough covered at all times. Dust each rolled-out portion lightly with cornstarch to prevent sticking and lay flat on board. Roll half of sheet nearest you away from you like a jelly roll; then roll half farthest from you toward center like a jelly roll to meet in center. With very sharp knife cut into desired widths (1/8 inch wide for most recipes, a bit wider for soup recipes). With blunt edge of knife lift at center fold and shake strips free. Loosen with fingers and dust with cornstarch as needed to prevent sticking. Place in well-covered container or plastic bag. Refrigerate up to 2 days or freeze. Defrost in refrigerator before using.

NOODLES

For 1 pound fresh noodles, substitute 1/2 pound dried noodles. As a rule, wheat or rice noodles may be used interchangeably for noodle dishes. Bean-thread noodles are treated the same as dried rice noodles (soak before parboiling) and may be used in soup and toss recipes, but not pan-fry recipes.

PARBOILING EGG OR WHEAT NOODLES

Bring a large pot of water to boil, salt lightly and add 1 teaspoon vegetable oil to prevent noodles from boiling over. Add the noodles, separating the strands and slipping into the boiling water gradually, stirring to prevent sticking. Bring water back to boil, lower heat to medium and cook until noodles are just barely tender. Cooking time depends upon type of noodle: fresh noodles only require about 2 minutes, dried 6 to 8 minutes. Remove from heat and drain immediately. Run cold water over and drain again. Toss with a little peanut oil or sesame oil to prevent sticking. Proceed with recipe.

HOMEMADE FUN
(Rice Noodle Skins)

2 cups rice flour
1/2 teaspoon powdered alum
1/2 teaspoon salt
2-3/4 cups water
peanut oil

Using a pastry board, place the rice flour in the center and sprinkle the alum and salt over it. Blend these dry ingredients together and then slowly add some of the water, a little at a time, along with 3 tablespoons of peanut oil. Add only enough water to make a ball of smooth dough and knead 10 minutes to give an elastic texture to the finished noodle. Place kneaded dough into a mixing bowl, break dough up with fingers and slowly add remaining water to make a batter, mixing in well. The batter should be very smooth and completely free of lumps. Let batter rest for 30 minutes. Oil a large pie pan and place on a rack over 2 inches of water in a large pot. Ladle enough batter into pie pan to cover surface. The amount of batter used will determine the thinness or thickness of the noodle. Cover pot and bring water to boil over high heat. Lower heat to medium and steam 15 minutes or until the noodle is set. When the noodle is cooked, remove pie pan from rack and have another oiled pan ready to repeat process until all the batter has been used. Let noodle cool in pan until it can be handled, roll it off onto a plate and set aside until all noodles are made. To make noodles, cut in 1/2-inch slices and separate.

Yield: 2 pounds

Note Rice noodle skins, called bok fun, may be purchased in Chinese take-out pastry shops. They can be used for making cold appetizers and hot noodle dishes.

PARBOILING RICE NOODLES

Fresh rice noodles (homemade fun, preceding, or purchased) are fully cooked and do not need parboiling. Dried rice noodles should be soaked in warm water 10 minutes to uncoil strands, then drained. Bring a large pot of water to boil, salt lightly and gradually add noodles. Return almost to boil, and test for doneness. Do not overcook or noodles will become mushy. Remove from heat, drain immediately and run noodles under cold water. Drain and toss with a little peanut or sesame oil to prevent sticking. Proceed with recipe.

PARBOILING BEAN-THREAD NOODLES

Treat the same as dried rice noodles, preceding.

PAN-FRIED RICE NOODLES

1/4 cup peanut oil
1 pound fresh rice noodles, or
1/2 pound dried rice noodles, parboiled

Heat oil in wok or skillet and add rice noodles, browning lightly and quickly, about 1 to 2 minutes. Be careful noodles do not break up too much. Over stirring and cooking will make them mushy and they will stick to the wok.

DEEP-FRIED RICE-STICK NOODLES (PY MEI FUN) OR BEAN-THREAD NOODLES

peanut oil for deep-frying
rice-stick noodles (py mei fun) or
    bean-thread noodles as needed

In a wok or skillet, heat peanut oil at least 1/2 inch deep. When very hot, drop a small handful of noodles into the oil. They will expand many times their original size in a few seconds. If not completely immersed in oil, turn them over. Remove with slotted spoon when lightly golden and set on rack to drain. Repeat with remaining noodles.

NOODLES

BASIC SOUP NOODLES

A favorite luncheon dish.

6 cups chicken, pork or beef stock
1 tablespoon soy sauce
1 pound fresh egg noodles, parboiled
1/2 teaspoon Oriental sesame oil
salt and pepper to taste
2 tablespoons chopped green onion

Bring stock and soy to boil; add noodles and heat through. Return almost to boil, remove from heat and blend in sesame oil, salt and pepper. Pour into individual bowls and garnish with green onions.

Variations

For a more complete meal, add to stock and cook just until tender: shredded meats or seafood; vegetables such as fresh green peas, snow peas, bean sprouts, water chestnuts, shredded Napa cabbage, bok choy, spinach, lettuce or watercress. Soup may also be topped just before serving with: shredded cooked meat such as poultry, beef, lamb or ham (Chinese barbecued pork is especially good); hard-cooked eggs, quartered; bean curd (cut in 1-inch cubes); vegetables such as cooked peas, bamboo shoots, bean sprouts, water chestnuts, cooked green beans, shredded spinach or Napa cabbage, mushrooms, preserved Szechwan cabbage, pickled or preserved vegetables; and chopped peanuts.

SOUP NOODLES WITH TREASURES FROM THE SEA

4 cups chicken stock
1 teaspoon fish soy
1 teaspoon dry sherry
8 raw shrimp, shelled and deveined
1/2 pound squid, cleaned, cut in half
    lengthwise and scored
1/2 cup thinly sliced canned abalone
1/2 cup thinly sliced bamboo shoots
1/4 cup thinly sliced water chestnuts
1/4 pound snow peas, or
1/2 cup fresh green peas
1/2 teaspoon Oriental sesame oil
salt and pepper to taste
1 pound fresh egg noodles, parboiled and
    kept hot
2 tablespoons minced green onion

Combine stock, soy and sherry and bring just to boil. Add seafood and vegetables and return just to the boil. Add sesame oil and salt and pepper to taste. Place hot noodles in large bowl. Pour soup over and garnish with green onion. Serve immediately.

Variation Rice noodles or bean-thread noodles may be substituted for the egg noodles.

BASIC WON TON SOUP

Usually served as a main meal, not as a soup course.

1 recipe pork and shrimp won ton filling
   (page 170)
1 pound won ton skins
8 cups basic chicken stock
2 green onions, chopped
1/2 teaspoon Oriental sesame oil
salt or light soy sauce to taste

Fill won ton skins and fold according to directions on page 172. Bring large pot of water to boil and gradually add half the filled won tons. Boil until they rise to surface and then continue cooking 1 more minute or until tender. Drain, run through cold water and drain again. Repeat with remaining filled won tons. Heat the stock just to boiling and add won tons. Heat through, add onions and sesame oil and salt or soy to taste. Serve immediately in large soup bowls.

Variations Any of the following may be added to the soup.

Sliced bamboo shoots, water chestnuts, mushrooms, Napa cabbage, bok choy (Chinese chard), spinach, bean sprouts

Shrimp, squid, canned sliced abalone, sliced chicken meat, gizzards and/or livers, Chinese sausage, ham

Any leftover cooked roast meats such as turkey, lamb, veal, beef or pork

Variation with Barbecued Pork When returning won tons to stock, add 1/2 pound sliced Chinese barbecued pork.

Variation with Beef Substitute beef stock for the chicken stock. Combine 1/2 pound thinly sliced flank steak with 1 tablespoon dark soy sauce or oyster sauce and 1 teaspoon rice wine or dry sherry. Stir-fry meat mixture in 2 tablespoons peanut oil until meat loses its redness. Top individual servings of soup with the meat garnish and fresh coriander leaves.

COLD NOODLES

A favorite of Peking, Hunan, Szechwan and Shanghai during the hot summer months.

COLD NOODLES
WITH MIXED VEGETABLES

1 pound fresh egg noodles, parboiled and
    chilled 2 hours
1/2 pound Chinese barbecued pork, shredded
1/2 pound bean sprouts, blanched 1 minute
1 cucumber, seeded and cut in matchstick
1/2 cup thinly sliced radishes
2 green onions, minced
light soy sauce
fish soy
hoisin sauce
red rice vinegar or red wine vinegar
Oriental sesame oil
chili oil

Divide cold noodles into individual servings. Top each serving with the pork, bean sprouts, cucumber, radishes and green onions. Serve remaining ingredients for guests to toss into their own dish of noodles.

COLD NOODLES WITH
CHICKEN AND PEANUTS
Peking

dressing of:
    1/4 cup water
    3 tablespoons sesame-seed paste or
        peanut butter
    3 tablespoons peanut oil
    3 tablespoons red rice vinegar or red
        wine vinegar
    1 teaspoon sugar
    3 tablespoons light soy sauce
    1 tablespoon Oriental sesame oil
1 pound fresh egg noodles, parboiled and
    chilled 2 hours
1 cup cooked, shredded chicken meat
1/2 cup chopped roasted peanuts
2 tablespoons toasted sesame seeds
1/4 cup minced green onion or chives

Combine dressing ingredients, blend well and set aside. Place chilled noodles on serving dish and top with chicken, peanuts, sesame seeds and green onions or chives. Drizzle dressing over and serve.

GUON FUN
(Rice Noodle Roll with Vegetables and Meat)

1 recipe homemade fun (page 72)
1 pound mung bean sprouts, blanched
   1 minute and well drained
1 cup shredded cooked chicken
egg slivers (page 50)
2 green onions, cut in thin lengthwise strips
coriander sprigs
1/2 cup thinly sliced tea melon
3 tablespoons slivered preserved ginger
2 tablespoons toasted sesame seeds
Oriental sesame oil
salt and pepper
soy sauce or oyster sauce

Place a round noodle skin on a sheet of wax paper. Starting in center of noodle, place a row of bean sprouts. Make layers of the chicken, egg slivers, green onion, coriander, tea melon and ginger on top of the bean sprouts. Sprinkle sesame seeds on top and season with a little sesame oil, salt and pepper. Be careful not to fill too generously or the noodle will be difficult to roll. Place half of circle nearest you over the filling and roll the noodle tightly. Put on a plate seam side down and repeat with remaining noodle skins and filling. Cut noodle rolls into 1-1/2-inch lengths and stand on plate cut side up. Serve at room temperature with soy or oyster sauce.
Variation Substitute Chinese barbecued pork for the chicken.

有栖行證廬江李呢

HOM FUN

1/2 cup dried shrimp, soaked to soften
   and minced
2 green onions, finely chopped
3 tablespoons toasted sesame seeds
1/2 teaspoon Oriental sesame oil
1 recipe homemade fun batter (page 72)

Combine shrimp, green onions, sesame seeds and sesame oil. Prepare fun batter and ladle into oiled pan as directed in recipe. Sprinkle about 1 tablespoon of shrimp mixture on top of batter before steaming. When noodle is cooked, allow to cool enough to handle, roll and slice in 1-inch pieces. Serve for dim sum or as appetizer.

NOODLES

CHOW MEIN
(Pan-Fried Noodles)

1 pound fresh wheat or egg noodles,
   parboiled, or
1/2 pound dried wheat or egg noodles,
   parboiled
4 to 7 tablespoons peanut oil
salt to taste

Be sure noodles are well drained and cool. Heat 4 tablespoons of the oil in a wok or skillet. When hot, add half the noodles, spreading out evenly. Reduce heat to medium and brown lightly. Turn over and brown other side. Remove to heatproof plate and keep warm in oven. Add more oil to skillet and repeat with remaining noodles. Toss noodles with a mixture of the following ingredients or with any stir-fry dish.

1 tablespoon hoisin sauce
1 tablespoon brown bean sauce
1 teaspoon Oriental sesame oil
2 tablespoons minced green onion or chives
chili oil to taste
1 cup slivered cooked meat of choice
1 cup blanched fresh green peas or snow peas

CURRY, TOMATO AND BEEF CHOW MEIN
Canton

1 recipe pan-fried noodles, preceding
1/2 pound flank or skirt steak, sliced thinly
   across grain
2 slices ginger root, minced
1 garlic clove, minced
1 tablespoon soy sauce
3 tablespoons peanut oil
1/2 onion, cut into 1-inch chunks
1/2 bell pepper, cut into 1-inch chunks
1 tablespoon curry powder
1 pound firm ripe tomatoes, cut in 6 or
   8 wedges
1 teaspoon sugar
1/2 teaspoon salt
binder of:
   1 tablespoon water
   2 teaspoons cornstarch
coriander sprigs

Prepare noodles and keep warm. Combine meat, ginger root, garlic and soy sauce. Heat 2 tablespoons of the peanut oil in a wok or skillet. Stir-fry meat mixture 1 minute or until meat begins to lose its redness. Remove to plate and heat remaining oil. Stir-fry onion, bell pepper and curry powder 10 seconds. Add tomatoes, sugar and salt. Cover and let steam rise to surface, about 2 minutes. Return reserved meat to skillet, bind with cornstarch mixture and toss with noodles. Garnish with coriander sprigs.

LONG LIFE NOODLES
Peking

This is a traditional Peking noodle dish served on birthdays. The noodles represent long life and thus should never be cut.

1 pound long, thin fresh egg noodles, parboiled
1/2 cup peanut oil
1 pound lean ground pork butt
1/3 cup brown bean sauce
1 tablespoon sugar
1/2 cup minced green onions
1 tablespoon Oriental sesame oil

Prepare noodles and keep warm. Heat oil in wok or skillet and stir-fry pork until it loses its redness, about 2 to 3 minutes. Add brown bean sauce and stir-fry 3 minutes. Blend in sugar and cook another 2 minutes. Blend in onions and sesame oil and transfer to heated serving bowl. Place noodles on large serving platter to be served in individual bowls at the table. Pass the meat sauce and let each guest spoon the sauce over noodles. Sauce is intended to be oily.

Variations

Toss 1 cucumber, seeded and diced, with sauce.

When stir-frying brown bean sauce, add 1 cup diced bamboo shoots.

When stir-frying pork, add 2 or more dried red chili peppers.

When stir-frying pork, add 2 slices ginger root, minced, and 2 garlic cloves, minced.

五穀之長
盛德之徵

RICE NOODLES WITH
STIR-FRIED BEEF AND VEGETABLES

1/2 pound flank or skirt steak, sliced
   thinly across grain
1 garlic clove, minced
1 slice ginger root, minced
1 tablespoon soy sauce
1 tablespoon oyster sauce
3 tablespoons peanut oil
1 pound vegetable of choice*
1/4 cup water
1/2 teaspoon Oriental sesame oil
1 pound pan-fried rice noodles (page 73)
salt to taste

Combine meat, garlic, ginger, soy and oyster sauce. Heat 2 tablespoons of the peanut oil in wok or skillet. Stir-fry meat mixture 30 seconds or until meat starts to lose its redness. Remove to plate and heat remaining peanut oil in wok. Stir-fry vegetable 30 seconds. Add water (omit if using leafy vegetable), cover and let steam rise to surface. Do not over-cook. Return beef to wok and add sesame oil and noodles. Toss to blend well and add salt to taste. Remove to heated platter.

*Asparagus, sliced in 1/2-inch diagonal slices; bean sprouts; Chinese broccoli, cut in 2-inch pieces; bok choy (Chinese chard), cut in 2-inch pieces.

GREEN ONION PANCAKES
Hunan

3 cups unbleached flour
1 cup boiling water
1/4 cup cold water
1/4 cup peanut oil
2 tablespoons Oriental sesame oil
1/4 cup chopped green onions
1 tablespoon salt
peanut oil for frying

Measure flour into a bowl. Gradually add the boiling water, stirring constantly with chopsticks or fork to blend well. Let cool to lukewarm and add cold water. Knead on lightly floured board until smooth and elastic, at least 10 minutes. Cover with tea towel and let dough rest 30 minutes. Divide dough into 6 or 8 pieces. Roll each piece into a 10-inch round. Combine the peanut oil and sesame oil and brush each round with oil mixture and sprinkle each with 1-1/2 teaspoons green onions. Dust lightly with salt. Roll each round up tightly like a jelly roll, tucking in ends to prevent oil and onions from spilling out. Form into coil shape, tucking end into center. Press down flat and roll out 1/4 inch thick into a circle to fit a large skillet. To fry, heat 2 tablespoons peanut oil in skillet, lower heat to medium and fry each pancake until golden. Turn and add another tablespoon of oil. Fry until golden. Shake pan while frying to create a flakier pastry. Remove each pancake and keep warm in oven while repeating with remaining circles. Cut into wedges and serve.

CHINESE PANCAKES

These are thin pancakes similar to a flour tortilla. They are also known as Mandarin pancakes or Peking doilies.

3/4 cup boiling water
2 cups unbleached flour
peanut oil or Oriental sesame oil

Gradually add boiling water to the flour, blending well with chopsticks or fork. Turn out onto floured board, knead 3 to 5 minutes and form into ball. Dough should be soft but not sticky. Cover with dampened tea towel and let rest 30 minutes. Knead again for 1 minute and with hands roll dough into a 1-1/2-inch thick rope. Cut into 16 equal pieces and flatten each piece to 1/2-inch thickness. Brush a little peanut or sesame oil on top of each round. Place one oiled round on top of another oiled round, oiled sides together. Roll out evenly and thinly to a 5- to 7-inch round. Heat an ungreased crêpe pan or skillet and cook rounds one at a time for 30 seconds per side. The pancake is ready to turn when small golden spots appear on the underside. Do not allow to brown. Immediately remove from heat, separate the joined halves and stack on plate. Cover with tea towel or aluminum foil until all rounds have been cooked.
Yield: 16 pancakes
Note May be made ahead of time, stacked and wrapped in aluminum foil, then steamed 10 minutes or until heated through. If freezing, add 10 minutes to steaming time.

NOODLES

81

VEGETABLES

MIXED VEGETABLE PICKLE
Szechwan

2 pounds cucumbers, seeded
2 pounds each carrots and turnips
1 pound cabbage
8 cups boiling water
1/3 cup salt
2 tablespoons Szechwan peppercorns, crushed
6 slices ginger root
6 or more dried red chili peppers, crushed
1/4 cup rice wine

Cut cucumbers, carrots and turnips into 1-1/2 by 1/2-inch slices. Cut cabbage into 1-1/2-inch pieces. Set vegetables aside. In a 1-gallon crock, combine water, salt and peppercorns. Let cool and add remaining ingredients and reserved vegetables. Cover crock and let stand at room temperature 3 days. Refrigerate.
Note Brine may be re-used and replenished with additional vegetables. As fresh vegetables are added, add 2 additional teaspoons salt and 2 additional tablespoons wine.

SWEET PICKLED VEGETABLES
Canton

3 cups diagonally sliced (1/8 inch) carrots
1 large bell pepper, cut in 1-inch chunks
1 sweet red pepper, cut in 1-inch chunks
2 onions, cut in 1-inch chunks
1 unpeeled cucumber, seeded and cut
   in 1-inch chunks
1/2 cup thinly sliced ginger root
2 or more dried red chili peppers
1 cup rice vinegar
1 cup sugar
1/2 teaspoon salt
1 cup water

Prepare vegetables and set aside. Combine ginger root, chili peppers, vinegar, sugar, salt and water in a saucepan; bring to rapid boil, lower heat and simmer 5 minutes. Remove from heat, cool to lukewarm and add carrots. Cool completely, stirring occasionally. Add remaining vegetables and pour into jars. Refrigerate covered at least 4 hours or overnight. May be stored in refrigerator up to 1 week.
Yield: 3 pints

VEGETABLES

WHITE TURNIP PICKLE
Peking

2 pounds Chinese turnips or daikon
3 tablespoons salt
4 cups boiling water
2 or more dried red chili peppers
4 slices ginger root

Peel turnips and cut into slices 1/2 inch thick and 1-1/2 inches long. Place in glass jars or a 2-quart crock. Combine remaining ingredients, bring to boil and let cool. Pour over turnips and let stand at room temperature 24 hours. Refrigerate 24 hours before serving. Yield: 2 quarts

CHINESE MUSTARD GREEN PICKLE
Canton

2 quarts Chinese mustard green stalks
   (about 4 to 5 pounds mustard greens)
1/4 cup salt
boiling water
2 cups white vinegar
2 cups water
1 cup sugar
6 slices ginger root

Clean mustard green stalks and cut into 1-inch diagonal chunks, reserving leafy greens for soup. Sprinkle salt over stalks and let stand 2 hours. Rinse salt off and pour boiling water over. Drain immediately, cool and place in glass jars. Combine remaining ingredients, bring to boil and simmer 5 minutes. Let cool. Pour over vegetables, cover and store in refrigerator at least 2 days.
Yield: 2 quarts

AGAR-AGAR SALAD
Peking

4 ounces noodle-type agar-agar
2 tablespoons fish soy
1 teaspoon Oriental sesame oil
1 tablespoon rice vinegar
1 teaspoon sugar
2 green onions, cut in 2-inch lengths, then
   in matchstick
2 carrots, cut in 2-inch lengths, then
   in matchstick
1 cucumber, seeded and cut in 2-inch
   lengths, then in matchstick
2 tablespoons toasted sesame seeds

Soak agar-agar in cold water 2 minutes to just inflate. Drain, wash in cold water and drain again. Combine with fish soy, sesame oil, vinegar and sugar. Toss with vegetables and sprinkle with sesame seeds. Serve at room temperature or chilled.

MUNG BEAN SPROUT SALAD
Hunan

1 pound mung bean sprouts
1 tablespoon light soy sauce
1 teaspoon Oriental sesame oil
1 tablespoon rice vinegar
2 tablespoons minced green onion
2 tablespoons toasted sesame seeds
2 or more dried red chili peppers, crushed, or
1/2 teaspoon chili oil

Toss ingredients together well. Adjust seasonings to taste and chill.

SOUR-HOT NAPA CABBAGE RELISH
Hunan

5 pounds Napa cabbage, cut into 1-1/2-inch
   pieces (choose firm white heads)
1/2 cup salt
3 tablespoons minced garlic
2 tablespoons minced ginger root
4 or more dried red chili peppers, crushed

Sprinkle cabbage with salt and let stand 4
hours until cabbage is wilted. Drain off excess
water and combine cabbage with remaining
ingredients. Pack into glass jars or crock, filling to within 2 inches from top. Add cold
water just to cover cabbage. Cover jars loosely
so cabbage will ferment. Let sit at room temperature 2 to 3 days. Check on second day for
saltiness, adding more salt if necessary. Bubbles will rise to surface and cabbage will have
a sour taste when ready to eat. Cover jars with
tight-fitting lids and refrigerate.
Yield: 3 quarts

SPICY CUCUMBER RELISH
Szechwan

4 unpeeled cucumbers
2 tablespoons salt
4 garlic cloves, thinly sliced
1 teaspoon Szechwan peppercorns, crushed
1 tablespoon hot bean paste
1 teaspoon chili oil
2 teaspoons sugar
1 tablespoon rice vinegar
1 tablespoon Oriental sesame oil

Cut cucumbers lengthwise in 4 strips; remove
seeds and cut strips into 2-inch lengths. Place
in bowl and toss with salt. Let stand 2 hours,
rinse with cold water and pat dry. Combine
remaining ingredients and toss well with cucumbers. Marinate at room temperature at
least 3 hours. Chill before serving.

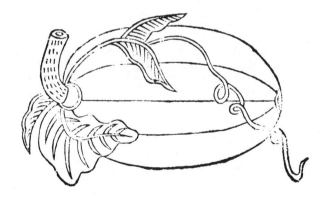

VEGETABLES

MARINATED LOTUS ROOT

1 pound fresh, firm lotus root
3 tablespoons rice vinegar
3 tablespoons light soy sauce
2 teaspoons sugar
2 teaspoons Oriental sesame oil
2 tablespoons peanut oil
1/2 teaspoon chili oil
2 tablespoons toasted sesame seeds

Peel and slice lotus root into very thin cross-wise slices. Soak for 15 minutes in cold water. Drain, dip into boiling water for only 10 seconds and immediately plunge into cold water. Drain and set aside. Combine remaining ingredients except sesame seeds and toss with lotus root. Chill 1 hour and serve sprinkled with sesame seeds.

SWEET AND SOUR CABBAGE
Szechwan

2 pounds Napa or white cabbage
5 tablespoons peanut oil
3 or more dried red chili peppers, seeds removed
1 teaspoon Szechwan peppercorns, crushed
3 tablespoons soy sauce
2 tablespoons sugar
1 teaspoon salt
2 tablespoons rice vinegar
1 tablespoon Oriental sesame oil

Cut cabbage in pieces 1-1/2 inches long and 1 inch wide. Set aside. Heat peanut oil in wok or skillet and stir-fry chili peppers until brown; add peppercorns and cabbage and stir-fry 3 minutes or until cabbage is just heated through. Combine remaining ingredients and toss with cabbage. Serve hot or cold.

EGGPLANT WITH PEANUT BUTTER
Shantung

1 1-pound eggplant
2 tablespoons peanut oil
2 garlic cloves, minced
1 slice ginger root, minced
1 tablespoon peanut butter or
    sesame-seed paste
1/2 teaspoon salt
1/2 cup water
1/2 teaspoon Oriental sesame oil

Peel eggplant, cut in 1-inch chunks and set aside. Heat oil in a wok or skillet and stir-fry garlic and ginger 20 seconds. Add eggplant and stir-fry another 20 seconds. Blend in peanut butter, salt and water. Cover, bring to boil, lower heat to medium and cook 5 to 7 minutes until eggplant is tender. Stir in sesame oil and serve. May also be served at room temperature.

VEGETABLES

VEGETABLES

STIR-FRIED VEGETABLES

A good stir-fry vegetable dish must have just the right amount of moisture. High moisture-content vegetables require little or no additional liquid during cooking. Low moisture-content vegetables require the addition of about 1/3 cup of liquid to create steam. The vegetable is always added to the heated wok or skillet with oil and stirred and tossed quickly to coat it well. This retains as much of the natural fresh flavor and vibrant color of the vegetable as possible.

HIGH MOISTURE-CONTENT VEGETABLES AND CUTTING METHODS

bok choy: cut in 2-inch lengths
Chinese mustard greens: green tops cut in
    2-inch lengths; stems, if thick, cut in
    1/2-inch diagonal slices
cabbage, head or Napa: coarsely shred
cucumber: thinly slice
lettuce: coarsely shred
mung bean sprouts
onions, green: cut in 2-inch lengths
onions, Spanish: cut in 1-inch chunks, thinly
    slice or dice
soybean sprouts
spinach: leave whole or halve if large
Swiss chard: cut in 2-inch lengths
tomatoes: cut in wedges
watercress: leave whole or cut in half

LOW MOISTURE-CONTENT VEGETABLES AND CUTTING METHODS

asparagus: slice diagonally, 1/2 inch thick
bamboo shoots: thinly slice, cut in
    matchstick or dice
bell pepper: cut in 1-inch chunks,
    thinly slice or dice
bitter melon: cut in 1-inch chunks or
    slice diagonally 1/4 inch thick
broccoli, American or Chinese: cut in
    2-inch flowerets; slice stems 1/4 inch thick
Brussels sprouts: leave whole or halve if large
carrots: thinly slice, cut in matchstick or dice
cauliflower: cut in 2-inch flowerets;
    slice stems 1/4 inch thick
celery: slice 1/4 inch thick on diagonal or
    in 1/2-inch dice
eggplant: cut in 1-inch chunks
fuzzy melon: thinly slice
kohlrabi: thinly slice, cut in matchstick or
    in 1/2-inch dice
lotus root: halve crosswise to expose holes
    and slice 1/8 to 1/4 inch thick
mushrooms, dried or fresh: thinly slice, shred
    or cut in 1/2-inch dice
okra, American or Chinese: cut in 1-inch
    rolling cut
peas
potatoes and other starchy, root vegetables
    such as yams, taro, etc: cut in 1/4-inch
    thick slices or in 1/2-inch dice

snow peas: leave whole or halve if large

squash, hard or winter: cut in 1/4-inch thick slices or in 1/2-inch dice

string beans and Chinese long beans: snapped or cut in 2-inch lengths

turnips: cut in 1/4-inch thick slices or in 1/2-inch dice

water chestnuts: thinly slice or in 1/4-inch dice

winter melon: cut in 1/4-inch thick slices or in 1/2-inch dice

zucchini: cut in 1-inch rolling cut or 1/4-inch diagonal slices

BASIC STIR-FRIED VEGETABLES

1 pound vegetable of choice
2 tablespoons peanut oil
1/2 teaspoon salt
2 slices ginger root (optional)
1 garlic clove, bruised (optional)
1 to 2 tablespoons soy sauce
about 1/3 cup stock or water (depending upon vegetable, see page 88)
1/2 teaspoon sugar
1/2 teaspoon Oriental sesame oil (optional)

Prepare vegetable according to directions on page 88. Set aside. Heat peanut oil in a wok or skillet over high heat and add salt, ginger root and garlic. Stir-fry 5 to 10 seconds until pungent. Add vegetables and stir-fry an additional 10 seconds to coat well with oil. Lower heat to medium if necessary to prevent scorching. Add soy sauce, stock or water and sugar. Continue stir-frying until vegetables are just heated through; or cover and let steam rise to surface. Cooking time varies with the cut, age and variety of vegetables. Greens should be tender but still crunchy. Tomatoes should not lose their shape entirely and take about 1 to 3 minutes. Firmer vegetables require slightly more cooking time, about 2 to 5 minutes, again depending upon cut, age and variety. Toss in sesame oil.

Variations

Substitute 2 tablespoons chicken or bacon fat for the peanut oil.

Season hot oil with 2 or more dried red chili peppers when stir-frying ginger and garlic.

Add 1 teaspoon sugar and 1 tablespoon vinegar when adding stock or water for sweet and sour stir-fry.

Sprinkle cooked vegetables with toasted sesame seeds or chopped peanuts, almonds or walnuts.

Omit soy sauce. Drizzle with a little oyster sauce just before serving.

Suggested Combinations

1/2 pound bean sprouts and 1/2 pound asparagus, sliced on diagonal

1 cup sliced bamboo shoots, 1 cup sliced carrots or kohlrabi, 1/2 bell pepper, sliced

1/2 pound Napa cabbage, shredded, 2 green onions, cut in 2-inch lengths, 4 to 6 dried forest mushrooms, soaked to soften and thinly sliced

V
E
G
E
T
A
B
L
E
S

VEGETABLES

STIR-FRIED VEGETABLES WITH BROWN BEAN SAUCE

Especially good with asparagus, bamboo shoots, bean sprouts, broccoli, carrots, cauliflower, celery, cucumber, string beans and zucchini.

1 pound vegetable of choice
2 tablespoons peanut oil
1 slice ginger root (optional)
1 garlic clove, bruised (optional)
1 tablespoon brown bean sauce
2 teaspoons soy sauce
1/2 teaspoon sugar
about 1/3 cup water (depending upon
    vegetable, see page 88)
1/2 teaspoon Oriental sesame oil

Cut vegetable as directed on page 88. Set aside. Heat peanut oil in wok or skillet and stir-fry ginger and garlic 10 seconds until pungent. Add brown bean sauce and vegetable and stir-fry 10 seconds to coat vegetable with oil and brown bean sauce. Add soy, sugar and water. Cover and let steam rise to surface. Lower heat if necessary and cook until vegetable is just tender crisp. Toss in sesame oil.
Variation with Ham Toss 1/4 pound cooked slivered ham into wok with the sesame oil.

STIR-FRIED VEGETABLES WITH BLACK BEAN SAUCE

Especially good with asparagus, bell pepper, bitter melon, kohlrabi, any squash (including zucchini), tomatoes, potatoes, yams, taro root, eggplant and cauliflower.

1 pound vegetable of choice
2 tablespoons fermented black beans,
    rinsed and mashed
1 slice ginger root, minced
1 garlic clove, minced
2 tablespoons peanut oil
2 teaspoons soy sauce
1 teaspoon rice wine or dry sherry
1/2 teaspoon sugar
about 1/3 cup water (depending upon
    vegetable, see page 88)

Cut vegetable as directed on page 88. Set aside. Combine fermented black beans, ginger and garlic. Heat peanut oil in a wok or skillet and stir-fry black bean mixture 10 seconds. Add vegetable and stir-fry to coat with oil and black bean mixture, about 10 seconds. Add soy, wine, sugar and water. Cover and let steam rise to surface. Cook just until vegetable is heated through and tender crisp.
Variation with Beef When stir-frying black bean mixture, add 1/4 pound lean ground beef. Stir-fry 15 seconds before proceeding with the recipe.

STIR-FRIED VEGETABLES WITH FERMENTED BEAN CAKE

Especially good with asparagus, bean sprouts, bok choy (Chinese chard), broccoli, any kind of cabbage, kohlrabi, string beans, Brussels sprouts, squash (including zucchini), eggplant, lettuce, spinach and watercress.

1 pound vegetable of choice
2 tablespoons peanut oil
1 garlic clove, bruised
1 tablespoon fermented bean cake
1 tablespoon liquid from fermented bean cake
about 1/3 cup water (depending upon
   vegetable, see page 88)
1/2 teaspoon sugar
salt to taste

Cut vegetables according to directions on page 88. Set aside. Heat peanut oil in a wok or skillet and stir-fry garlic until pungent and golden. Add fermented bean cake and stir constantly for 10 seconds. Add vegetable and stir-fry to coat well with oil and bean cake. Add bean cake liquid, water and sugar. Lower heat if necessary to prevent scorching. Cover and let steam rise to surface. Cook just until vegetable is tender crisp. Add salt to taste.
Variation with Pork As soon as garlic is pungent and golden, add 1/4 pound ground pork butt. Continue stir-frying 1 minute before adding bean cake and proceeding with recipe.

V
E
G
E
T
A
B
L
E
S

VEGETABLES

FIVE-TREASURE VEGETABLE STIR-FRY
Buddhist

3 tablespoons peanut oil
1/4 cup chopped green onions
2 slices ginger root, minced
1 cup diced bamboo shoots
1/2 cup diced water chestnuts
1/2 cup golden needles, soaked to soften
    and cut in half
1/2 cup cloud ears, soaked to soften
6 to 8 dried forest mushrooms, soaked to
    soften and diced
2 tablespoons light soy sauce
1/2 teaspoon each salt and sugar
1/4 cup water
1/2 teaspoon Oriental sesame oil
binder of:
    1 tablespoon water
    1 teaspoon cornstarch

Heat peanut oil in wok or skillet. When hot, stir-fry onion and ginger 10 seconds. Add bamboo shoots, water chestnuts, golden needles, cloud ears and mushrooms. Stir-fry 1 minute and add soy, salt, sugar, water and sesame oil. Cook over medium heat, covered, 5 minutes. Bind with cornstarch mixture and serve immediately.

STIR-FRIED VEGETABLES WITH HOISIN SAUCE

1 tablespoon light soy sauce
2 teaspoons hoisin sauce
1/2 teaspoon salt
1/2 teaspoon sugar
1/2 cup water
2 tablespoons peanut oil
1/4 pound snow peas
1 cup sliced bamboo shoots
1 celery rib, thinly sliced on diagonal
1 cup thinly sliced carrots, blanched 1 minute
1 small onion, sliced
2 tablespoons toasted sesame seeds

Combine soy, hoisin sauce, salt, sugar and water. Set aside. Heat peanut oil in a wok or skillet and stir-fry vegetables 10 seconds to coat well with oil. Add soy mixture and blend well. Cover, let steam rise to surface and cook until vegetables are just tender crisp. Transfer to heated serving dish and sprinkle with sesame seeds.
Variations Chinese okra, water chestnuts, asparagus, dried forest mushrooms or fresh mushrooms and bean sprouts may be added to or substituted for the vegetables in the recipe.

MO SHU RO
(Mixed Vegetables with Eggs and Pork)

egg slivers (page 50)
1/4 cup peanut oil
1/2 pound lean pork butt, cut in shreds
2 tablespoons light soy sauce
1 tablespoon rice wine or dry sherry
1/2 cup golden needles, soaked to soften
6 wood ears, soaked to soften, tough ends
  removed, cut in shreds
4 dried forest mushrooms, soaked to soften
  and cut in shreds
1 cup matchstick-cut bamboo shoots
1/2 pound Napa cabbage, shredded
3 green onions, cut in 2-inch lengths
1/3 cup water
1/2 teaspoon sugar
1/2 teaspoon salt

binder of:
    1 tablespoon water
    1 teaspoon cornstarch
1/2 teaspoon Oriental sesame oil
1 recipe Chinese pancakes (page 81),
    kept warm

Prepare egg slivers and set aside. Heat peanut oil in a wok or skillet and stir-fry pork, soy and wine for 30 seconds. Add golden needles, wood ears, mushrooms, bamboo shoots, cabbage and green onions. Stir-fry another 30 seconds and add water, sugar and salt. Cover and let steam rise to surface, about 2 minutes. Bind with cornstarch mixture and add sesame oil and egg slivers. Heat through and transfer to heated platter. Serve with Chinese pancakes. Each person fills his own.

VEGETABLES

DRY-COOKED LONG BEANS
Szechwan

1-1/2 pounds long beans or string beans
1 cup peanut oil for deep-frying
1/4 pound ground pork butt
2 tablespoons dried shrimp, soaked to soften
    and minced (reserve 2 tablespoons soaking
    liquid)
2 slices ginger root, minced
1 tablespoon sugar
1 tablespoon soy sauce
1/2 teaspoon salt
2 teaspoons rice vinegar
1 teaspoon Oriental sesame oil
2 tablespoons chopped green onions

Trim beans and break or cut into 2- to 3-inch lengths. Heat oil in wok or skillet until it begins to smoke. Deep-fry beans in small batches 3 minutes until they begin to wrinkle. Remove and drain. Repeat with rest of beans and set aside. Pour off all but 2 tablespoons of oil from skillet. Heat the oil and stir-fry pork, shrimp and ginger 2 minutes. Add sugar, soy, salt, reserved shrimp liquid and reserved beans. Raise heat and stir-fry until all liquid has evaporated. Turn off heat and blend in vinegar, sesame oil and green onions. Serve hot or cold.

WALNUTS AND PEPPERS IN SWEET AND SOUR SAUCE
Shanghai

1/4 cup peanut oil
1 cup walnut halves, blanched to remove skins
1 small onion, cut in 1/2-inch dice
1 bell pepper, cut in 1/2-inch dice
1 sweet red pepper, cut in 1/2-inch dice
1/4 cup water
2 tablespoons vinegar
2 tablespoons sugar
2 tablespoons catsup
1 tablespoon light soy sauce
1/2 teaspoon salt
binder of:
    1 tablespoon water
    1 teaspoon cornstarch

Heat 2 tablespoons of the oil in wok or skillet and stir-fry walnuts 2 minutes or until golden. Remove with slotted spoon and set aside. Add remaining peanut oil to skillet and heat. Add onion and peppers. Stir-fry 30 seconds. Combine remaining ingredients except binder, add to skillet and bring to rapid boil. Add reserved walnuts, bind with cornstarch mixture and serve immediately.

STIR-FRIED BROCCOLI AND BACON

1-1/2 pounds Chinese or American broccoli
2 tablespoons soy sauce
1 tablespoon sugar
1 tablespoon rice wine or dry sherry
2 slices ginger root, minced
1/2 cup water
3 strips bacon, cut in 1-inch pieces
salt to taste
binder of:
    1 tablespoon water
    1 teaspoon cornstarch

Cut broccoli flowerets into 2-inch lengths; remove tough ends and cut tender part of stems into 1/2-inch diagonal slices. Blanch 30 seconds (do not allow water to return to boil) and drain immediately. (Broccoli will be undercooked.) Combine soy, sugar, wine, ginger and water. Set aside. Heat a wok or skillet and add bacon. Fry 30 seconds to release fat; do not brown. Add broccoli and stir-fry to coat with fat. Add soy mixture, cover and let steam rise to surface just to heat through. Salt to taste and bind with cornstarch mixture.

95

VEGETABLES

BAMBOO SHOOTS, MUSHROOMS AND CUCUMBERS
Buddhist

2 tablespoons peanut oil
1 slice ginger root, minced
1 cup matchstick-cut bamboo shoots
6 dried forest mushrooms, soaked to
    soften and cut in matchstick
3 tablespoons light soy sauce
1 teaspoon sugar
1 cup matchstick-cut seeded cucumber
1/2 teaspoon Oriental sesame oil

Heat peanut oil in a wok or skillet and stir-fry ginger 1 minute. Add bamboo shoots, mushrooms, soy and sugar; stir-fry 2 minutes. Add cucumber and continue stir-frying over high heat 1 minute. Do not overcook. Add sesame oil and serve.

BRAISED SOYBEAN SPROUTS
Shanghai

2 tablespoons peanut oil
1/4 cup diced Virginia ham
1 pound soybean sprouts
1 tablespoon light soy sauce
1 teaspoon sugar
1/2 cup water
2 tablespoons chopped green onion
salt

Heat oil in a wok or skillet and stir-fry ham 30 seconds. Add soybean sprouts and stir-fry another 30 seconds. Blend in soy, sugar and water. Cover, bring just to boil, lower heat and simmer 5 minutes. Add green onion and salt to taste.

MOCK FISH
Buddhist

In this recipe, the potato represents the fish.

1 large potato, cooked, peeled and sliced
   1/4 inch thick
2 tablespoons flour
peanut oil for frying
1 small onion, sliced
1/2 pound snow peas
10 wood ears, soaked to soften, tough
   ends removed, cut in slivers
1/2 teaspoon salt
1/2 teaspoon sugar
1/3 cup water

Sprinkle potatoes with flour and deep-fry until golden. Drain and set aside. Pour off all but 2 tablespoons of the oil, reheat and add onion. Stir-fry 10 seconds and add snow peas and wood ears. Stir-fry another 10 seconds and add salt, sugar and water. Bring to rapid boil, stirring constantly, and cook until peas are just tender crisp. Add reserved fried potato slices, heat through and serve.

SPINACH, PEKING STYLE

1 pound spinach
2 tablespoons peanut oil
1/2 cup dried shrimp, soaked to soften
1 teaspoon Oriental sesame oil
2 tablespoons light soy sauce
1 teaspoon sugar
1/2 teaspoon salt
1/2 teaspoon mustard, dissolved in
1 tablespoon rice vinegar
1 tablespoon sesame-seed paste
2 tablespoons chopped green onion
1 slice ginger root, chopped
1/2 teaspoon chili oil

Blanch spinach just to wilt; drain, press out excess moisture, chop and cool. Place chopped spinach in serving bowl and set aside. Heat peanut oil in a wok or skillet and stir-fry shrimp 2 minutes. Combine shrimp with remaining ingredients and toss with spinach. Serve hot or cold.

VEGETABLES

VEGETABLES

EGGPLANT HUNAN STYLE

1 pound Japanese eggplants, or
1 1-pound eggplant
1/4 cup peanut oil
2 garlic cloves, minced
1 teaspoon minced ginger root
1 tablespoon hot bean paste
1 tablespoon soy sauce
2 teaspoons sugar
1/2 cup chicken stock or water
1 tablespoon rice vinegar
1 teaspoon Oriental sesame oil
2 tablespoons chopped green onion

Trim eggplants, but do not peel. Cut into 1-inch chunks. Heat 3 tablespoons of the oil in a skillet; add eggplant, lower heat to medium and stir-fry 3 minutes or until soft. Remove from skillet and set aside. Heat remaining peanut oil in skillet and stir-fry garlic, ginger and bean paste 10 seconds. Add soy, sugar and stock. Bring to boil, add vinegar and reserved eggplant. Mix well with sauce and cook 1 minute until sauce is absorbed. Blend in sesame oil and green onion and serve. May also be served at room temperature.

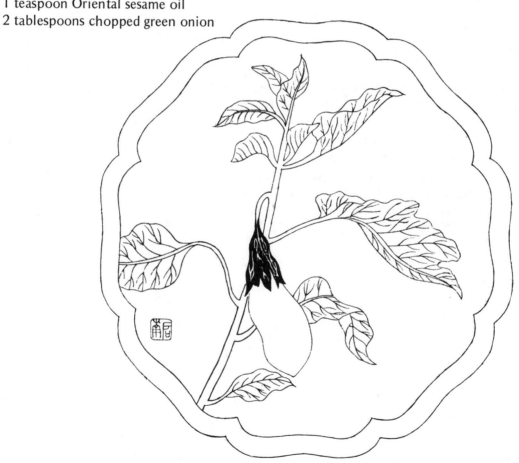

SZECHWAN-STYLE EGGPLANT

peanut oil for stir-frying
1 1-pound eggplant, peeled and cut in
   1-1/2-inch squares
1/4 pound ground pork butt
2 tablespoons chopped green onion
1 tablespoon each chopped garlic and
   ginger root
2 teaspoons hot bean paste
1 teaspoon each rice wine, soy sauce, sugar
   and rice vinegar
binder of:
   1 tablespoon water
   1 teaspoon cornstarch

Heat 3 tablespoons peanut oil in a wok or skillet and stir-fry eggplant squares 3 minutes or until soft. Remove and set aside. Stir-fry pork in 2 more tablespoons oil 1 minute. Add onion, garlic, ginger and hot bean paste. Stir-fry another minute. Add reserved eggplant and blend in wine, soy, sugar and vinegar. Bind with cornstarch mixture and serve.
Variation Omit hot bean paste; add 1 tablespoon peanut butter or sesame-seed paste.

FRIED EGGPLANT
Peking

1 1-pound eggplant
1/2 pound ground pork butt
1/2 cup cornstarch
2 tablespoons minced green onion
1 teaspoon light soy sauce
1 egg, beaten
bread crumbs
peanut oil for deep-frying
dipping sauce of:
   2 tablespoons light soy sauce
   1 tablespoon each rice wine and rice vinegar
   1/2 teaspoon sugar
   1/2 teaspoon Oriental sesame oil

Combine dipping sauce ingredients and set aside. Peel eggplant and cut into pieces 2 inches long and 1 inch thick. Make a slit in center of each piece. Combine pork, 1 tablespoon of the cornstarch, green onion and soy. Set aside. Rub eggplant inside and out with remaining cornstarch and stuff each slit with pork mixture. Dip one at a time in beaten egg and coat with bread crumbs. Deep fry in hot peanut oil until golden. Drain on paper toweling and serve hot with dipping sauce.

SEAFOOD

OYSTER SALAD
Canton

2 tablespoons peanut oil
1 pound lean pork butt, cut in 1/2-inch dice
1/4 teaspoon salt
1 tablespoon dark soy sauce
1 tablespoon oyster sauce
10 dried oysters, soaked 2 hours or more
    until soft, then well washed to remove sand
    and cut into 1/4-inch dice
10 medium-size dried forest mushrooms,
    soaked to soften and diced
1 cup diced bamboo shoots
1 cup diced water chestnuts
1 cup diced celery
1 piece tangerine peel, soaked to soften
    and minced
1/2 teaspoon five-spice powder
2 tablespoons rice wine or dry sherry
1 cup basic chicken stock or water
binder of:
    2 tablespoons water
    1 tablespoon cornstarch
Napa cabbage, butter or iceberg lettuce

Heat peanut oil in a wok or skillet and stir-fry
pork 1 minute to brown quickly. Add salt,
soy and oyster sauce, stir to coat well and
add oysters. Stir-fry 1 minute, add mushrooms and cook 1 minute. Blend in bamboo
shoots, water chestnuts, celery, tangerine
peel, five-spice powder, wine and stock. Cover
and simmer 20 minutes. Bind with cornstarch
mixture and serve hot or warm. May be made
ahead and reheated. To serve, spoon oyster
mixture into cabbage or lettuce leaves and eat
with fingers.

PEPPERY CLAMS
Peking

2 pounds fresh clams or mussels,
    well scrubbed
1/2 cup light soy sauce
2 garlic cloves, minced
2 or more dried red chili peppers, crushed
1 tablespoon rice vinegar
1 teaspoon sugar
2 tablespoons rice wine or dry sherry

Place clams in heatproof bowl and steam over
boiling water 8 minutes or until shells open.
Remove from heat, mix in remaining ingredients and marinate 4 hours in refrigerator.
Serve cold.

101

MARINATED ABALONE
Peking

1 1-pound can abalone, drained
1/2 cup light soy sauce
2 tablespoons rice vinegar
1 teaspoon sugar
1/2 teaspoon Oriental sesame oil

Slice abalone into thin strips. Combine remaining ingredients and marinate abalone slices 1 hour. Chill before serving.
Variations Unpeeled cucumber, seeded and sliced into thin strips, may be added just before serving. If desired, garnish with minced green onions or toasted sesame seeds. For spicier sauce, add 1/2 teaspoon of chili oil to marinade.

RAW FISH AND NOODLE SALAD
Canton

1 pound very fresh firm white fish fillet, cut in thin strips
1 tablespoon Oriental sesame oil
1 tablespoon peanut oil
1/2 teaspoon white pepper
1/4 teaspoon cinnamon
6 pickled scallions, slivered
2 green onions, cut in very thin matchstick
1 cucumber, peeled, seeded and cut in very thin matchstick
1 carrot, cut in very thin matchstick
6 coriander sprigs, cut in 2-inch lengths
1/2 cup tea melons, cut in matchstick
1/4 cup matchstick-cut preserved ginger
4 ounces rice-stick noodles (py mei fun), deep-fried (page 73)
shredded iceberg lettuce
2 tablespoons toasted sesame seeds
juice of 1 lemon

Combine fish, oils, pepper and cinnamon. Marinate 15 minutes. Toss with pickled scallions, onions, cucumber, carrot, coriander, tea melons, ginger and two-thirds of the fried rice-stick noodles. Place on bed of iceberg lettuce and garnish with remaining rice-stick noodles and sesame seeds. Sprinkle with lemon juice and serve immediately. Never toss and combine with noodles until ready to serve or noodles will lose their crispness.

MARINATED SQUID
Chekiang

1 pound fresh squid, cleaned
1-1/2 cups water
1/2 teaspoon salt
2 green onions, cut up
1 slice ginger root
1 tablespoon rice wine
2 tablespoons light soy sauce
1/2 teaspoon sugar
1/2 teaspoon Oriental sesame oil
1 tablespoon rice vinegar
salt and white pepper to taste
chopped green onions
coriander sprigs
bell pepper strips

Cut squid in half lengthwise and score inside surface in crisscross diagonal slices without cutting through. Bring water, salt, green onions, ginger root and wine to boil. Add squid and cook 2 minutes until squid curl. Do not overcook. Remove from heat and drain, reserving liquid for soup stock base. Combine soy sauce, sugar, sesame oil, vinegar and salt and pepper. Pour over squid and let cool. Chill. Garnish with green onions, coriander sprigs and bell pepper just before serving.

SPICED FISH
Chekiang

1 pound white fish fillets
1 tablespoon minced ginger root
2 green onions, chopped
2 tablespoons light soy sauce
1 tablespoon rice wine or dry sherry
6 tablespoons peanut oil
1/2 teaspoon five-spice powder
2 tablespoons sugar
1/4 cup boiling water

Select firm fish fillets and cut them into pieces approximately 1/2 inch thick by 1 inch by 3 inches. Marinate 2 to 3 hours in mixture of ginger root, green onions, soy and wine. Heat oil in heavy skillet. Drain fish slices, reserving marinade, and fry until brown on both sides. Drain on paper toweling. Remove oil from skillet. Combine five-spice powder, sugar and water. Add to skillet and stir well. Return fish to skillet with reserved marinade and cook until sauce is reduced by one-half. Cool and serve at room temperature.

PHOENIX TAIL PRAWNS
AND SNOW PEAS
Peking

1 pound raw prawns
1/2 teaspoon salt
1/8 teaspoon baking soda
1 teaspoon cornstarch
1 unbeaten egg white
1/4 cup peanut oil
1/4 pound snow peas, or
1 cup fresh green peas
1 teaspoon rice wine or dry sherry
1/4 cup chicken stock or water
1/4 teaspoon white pepper

Shell and devein prawns, keeping tails intact. Rinse with cold water and pat dry. Combine with salt, baking soda, cornstarch and egg white. Heat oil in wok or skillet and stir-fry prawns 1 minute until they curl. Remove from skillet and set aside. Stir-fry peas 1 minute. Add wine, stock and pepper. Bring to steam, cover and cook until peas are just tender. Return prawns to wok, heat through and serve immediately.

Variations

Add 1/2 cup sliced water chestnuts with
   the peas
Substitute 1/2 cup each sliced bamboo shoots
   and carrots, 1 bell pepper, cut in chunks,
   or 2 cups mung bean sprouts for the peas

SHRIMP IN HOT AND SOUR SAUCE
Peking

1 pound raw shrimp, shelled and deveined,
   tails intact
1 teaspoon rice wine or dry sherry
1 egg, separated
4 tablespoons cornstarch
peanut oil for deep-frying
2 green onions, chopped
2 slices ginger root, minced
2 garlic cloves, minced
1 dried red chili pepper, minced
1 bell pepper, chopped
1 tablespoon each sugar, rice vinegar
   and catsup
1/2 cup water
1/2 teaspoon salt
binder of:
   2 teaspoons water
   1 teaspoon cornstarch

Combine shrimp with wine, egg white and 1 teaspoon of the cornstarch. Let stand 30 minutes. Stir in egg yolk and sprinkle with remaining cornstarch to coat shrimp well. Heat oil in wok or skillet and deep-fry shrimp a few at a time 30 seconds until just cooked. Do not overcook. Drain on paper toweling, transfer to heated platter and keep warm. Pour off all but 2 tablespoons of the oil from the pan and stir-fry onion, ginger root, garlic, dried chili pepper and bell pepper 1 minute. Blend in sugar, vinegar, catsup, water and salt. Bring just to boil and bind with cornstarch mixture. Pour over shrimp and serve immediately.

Sizzling Rice Variation Pour shrimp and sauce over freshly fried rice crusts, page 43.

SEAFOOD

STEAMED LIVE CRABS

Place live hard-shell crab on a rack or bowl above at least 2 inches of water. Cover pot and steam over briskly boiling water 20 minutes. (If using soft-shell, small crabs, steam only 10 minutes.) Remove from heat, let stand 5 minutes and separate body and claws from hard shell. Discard any soft spongy parts of crab and reserve the smooth yellow crab butter. Discard any brown-yellow liquid inside crab shell. Split body section in half or quarters if large, and crack claws. Serve with either of the following dipping sauces.

沙船

GINGER LEMON SAUCE

1 tablespoon minced ginger root
1 teaspoon sugar
1 tablespoon light soy sauce
1 tablespoon freshly squeezed lemon juice
1 tablespoon crab butter (optional)

Combine ingredients and blend well.

GREEN ONION SAUCE

1 green onion, minced
1 slice ginger root, minced
1 teaspoon salt
1/4 teaspoon white pepper
3 tablespoons peanut oil
1 tablespoon Oriental sesame oil

Combine green onion, ginger, salt and pepper in individual heatproof small dishes or in 1 larger dish. Heat peanut oil until very hot, just to smoking point. Pour hot oil over green onion mixture. It should sizzle. Serve immediately. Also good for white cut chicken.

OYSTERS WITH BLACK BEAN SAUCE
Canton

1 pint shucked oysters
3 tablespoons peanut oil
1-1/2 tablespoons fermented black beans, rinsed and mashed
1 garlic clove, minced
1 slice ginger root, minced
1 tablespoon light soy sauce or fish soy
1 teaspoon rice wine or dry sherry
binder of:
    1 tablespoon water
    1 teaspoon cornstarch
2 tablespoons minced green onion

Drain oysters, halve if large and set aside. Heat oil in wok or skillet and add black beans, garlic and ginger. Stir-fry 10 seconds and add oysters, soy and wine. Do not stir. Let oysters cook 30 seconds, then carefully lift and stir gently so they do not break. Continue cooking 1 to 2 minutes longer. Do not overcook. Bind with cornstarch mixture and add green onion.

STIR-FRY PRAWNS IN THEIR SHELLS
Canton

1 pound raw prawns
3 tablespoons peanut oil
1 tablespoon chopped ginger root
2 garlic cloves, minced
1 tablespoon light soy sauce
1 tablespoon rice wine or dry sherry
1/2 teaspoon salt
1/4 teaspoon white pepper
chopped green onions
coriander sprigs

Trim and wash prawns, leaving shells and tails intact. Pat dry. Heat oil in wok or skillet and stir-fry ginger and garlic 30 seconds. Add prawns and stir-fry 2 minutes to brown shells lightly. Add soy, wine, salt and pepper. Continue stir-frying 2 minutes or until prawns are just cooked. Transfer to heated platter and garnish with green onions and coriander sprigs. When eating, savor all the juices from the shells before removing shrimp meat; the shells impart an unusual flavor.
Variations Add with soy sauce:
2 tablespoons tomato catsup and
　2 teaspoons sugar
1 tablespoon brown bean sauce, hoisin sauce, oyster sauce, or fermented black beans, rinsed and mashed
1 teaspoon chili oil, or 2 or more dried red chili peppers, crushed

STUFFED CLAMS
Canton

2 dozen clams, well scrubbed
1/2 pound ground pork butt
1/4 cup minced water chestnuts
2 tablespoons minced Virginia ham (optional)
2 dried forest mushrooms, soaked to soften, drained and minced (optional)
1/2 teaspoon Oriental sesame oil
1/4 teaspoon white pepper
1 teaspoon rice wine or dry sherry
1 tablespoon cornstarch
2 slices ginger root, cut in fine shreds
1 cup reserved clam broth from steaming
1 tablespoon chopped green onion
1/2 teaspoon Oriental sesame oil
binder of:
　2 tablespoons water
　1 tablespoon cornstarch

Place clams in saucepan with 1 cup water. Cover, bring to rapid boil and boil until shells open. Remove clams from shells and reserve liquid and shells. Mince clams and combine with pork, water chestnuts, ham, mushrooms, 1/2 teaspoon sesame oil, pepper, wine and cornstarch. Stuff shells and place on shallow heatproof dish. Sprinkle with ginger and steam over boiling water 20 minutes. Heat reserved clam liquid with green onion, add sesame oil and bind with cornstarch mixture. Pour over stuffed clams and serve.

CLAMS WITH BLACK BEAN SAUCE
Canton

2 pounds fresh or salt water clams or mussels
3 tablespoons peanut oil
2 tablespoons fermented black beans,
   rinsed and mashed
2 slices ginger root, minced
2 garlic cloves, minced
1/4 pound ground pork butt
1 tablespoon rice wine or dry sherry
1 tablespoon soy sauce
1 bell pepper, cut in chunks
1/4 cup water
binder of:
   1 tablespoon water
   1 teaspoon cornstarch
2 green onions, chopped

Scrub clam shells well and let soak in cold water 20 minutes. Drain well and set aside. In wok or skillet, heat oil. Add black beans, ginger and garlic and stir-fry 10 seconds. Add pork and stir-fry 30 seconds. Add clams and stir-fry another minute. Add wine, soy, bell pepper and water. Cover, bring to boil and let steam until clams open, approximately 3 to 5 minutes. Bind with cornstarch mixture and add green onions. Serve immediately.

SEAFOOD

BASIC STIR-FRY CRAB
Canton

1 large live hard-shell crab (approximately
   2 pounds)
1/4 cup peanut oil
2 green onions, cut in 2-inch lengths
2 garlic cloves, bruised
3 slices ginger root
1 tablespoon fish soy or oyster sauce
1 tablespoon light soy sauce
1 tablespoon rice wine or dry sherry
1/2 cup crab butter or water
1 teaspoon Oriental sesame oil
coriander sprigs

Drop live crab into boiling water 2 minutes. Remove immediately and plunge into cold water. Drain. Clean crab as directed in recipe for steamed crab, page 106, reserving hard shell. Heat peanut oil in a wok or heavy skillet and stir-fry onion, garlic and ginger 30 seconds. Add crab pieces and shell and stir-fry 30 seconds, stirring well to coat crab with oil. Combine fish soy, soy sauce, wine and crab butter. Add to skillet and blend in well. Cover and let steam rise to surface, about 3 to 5 minutes. Add sesame oil and garnish with coriander.

Variation with Fermented Black Bean Sauce (Canton) Omit fish soy or oyster sauce in basic stir-fry crab recipe. Add 2 tablespoons fermented black beans, rinsed and mashed, when stir-frying the onions, garlic and ginger.

Variation with Brown Bean Sauce Substitute 1 tablespoon brown bean sauce for the light soy sauce.

Variation with Egg Binder Prepare any of the stir-fry crab recipes. Beat 1 egg lightly and stir into skillet the last few seconds of cooking just to bind juices. Serve immediately.

SWEET AND SOUR SQUID
Shanghai

1-1/2 pounds fresh squid, cleaned
1 tablespoon minced ginger root
1 tablespoon rice wine or dry sherry
2 tablespoons cornstarch
peanut oil for deep-frying
2 dried red chili peppers, crushed (optional)
2 garlic cloves, minced
1 tablespoon soy sauce
2 tablespoons sugar
2 tablespoons rice vinegar
binder of:
    1/2 cup water
    1 tablespoon cornstarch
1/2 teaspoon Oriental sesame oil
matchstick-cut preserved ginger
pickled scallions

Score squid bodies in 1/4-inch crisscross pattern and cut into 1-inch by 1-1/2-inch diagonal pieces. Combine with squid heads, ginger root, wine and cornstarch. In peanut oil deep-fry a few at a time until curled. Drain and set aside. Remove all but 1 tablespoon oil from skillet and stir-fry peppers and garlic 30 seconds. Combine soy sauce, sugar, vinegar, binder and sesame oil and add to pan. Let simmer 2 minutes. Add squid and just heat through. Transfer to heated platter and garnish with ginger and scallions.

BASIC STEAMED FISH

Any kind of fish may be steamed. If small, leave whole. Keep fish fillets in slices, preferably 1 inch thick.

1 pound fish
1 tablespoon light soy sauce or fish soy
1 teaspoon rice wine or dry sherry
2 teaspoons peanut oil
2 slices ginger root, cut in thin slivers
2 green onions, cut in 1-1/2-inch lengths,
    then slivered

Rub fish well on both sides with soy and wine and place in shallow heatproof dish. Sprinkle top surface with oil, ginger and green onions. Steam on rack above boiling water for 20 minutes.

Variation with Fermented Black Bean Sauce or Brown Bean Sauce Prepare basic steamed fish, reducing soy sauce to 1 teaspoon and adding 1 tablespoon mashed fermented black beans or 1 tablespoon brown bean sauce.

Variation with Forest Mushrooms Prepare basic steamed fish, omitting green onions and placing on top of fish before steaming, 4 forest mushrooms, soaked to soften and then slivered.

STRIPED BASS WITH BROWN BEAN SAUCE
Szechwan

1 whole striped bass or other firm white
    fish, about 2 pounds
2 tablespoons peanut oil
1/4 cup matchstick-cut bamboo shoots
4 dried forest mushrooms, soaked to soften
    in 1/2 cup water, drained and cut in
    matchstick, water reserved
1/4 cup chopped green onion
1 slice ginger root, minced
1 tablespoon light soy sauce
1 tablespoon brown bean sauce
1/2 teaspoon salt
2 teaspoons rice wine or dry sherry
1 tablespoon rice vinegar
1 teaspoon sugar
1/2 teaspoon chili oil
binder of:
    1/2 cup reserved mushroom water
    1 tablespoon cornstarch

Clean fish and pat dry. Make 3 or 4 diagonal slashes on each side. Place in poacher, cover with boiling water and cook over low heat 3 minutes. Remove poacher from heat and let fish stand in water 12 to 15 minutes. With a slotted spoon, transfer fish to plate and keep warm. Heat peanut oil in wok or skillet and stir-fry bamboo shoots, mushrooms, green onion and ginger 1 minute. Combine remaining ingredients, add and cook until thickened. Pour over fish and serve immediately.

WHOLE POACHED FISH
Canton

1 whole rock cod, bass or other firm white
   fish (about 2 pounds)
4 cups water
4 slices ginger root
2 green onions
1 teaspoon salt
1 tablespoon each fish soy and light
   soy sauce
1/4 teaspoon pepper
1/4 cup peanut oil heated with:
   dash of Oriental sesame oil
   1 slice ginger root
   1 garlic clove
garnish of:
   slivered green onions
   coriander sprigs
   slivered preserved ginger
   slivered pickled scallions
   slivered tea melon

Place fish on a rack in a poacher or roasting
pan. Put water in a saucepan; add ginger,
green onion and salt and boil 5 minutes. Slowly pour over fish, adding more water if needed
to cover fish. Cover poacher and cook gently
over lowest heat 10 to 15 minutes. Remove
fish with slotted spoon to heated platter.
Sprinkle with fish soy, soy sauce and pepper.
Drizzle sizzling hot oil over and garnish.

WHOLE FRIED FISH
Shanghai

1 whole rock cod, perch or other firm white
    fish (about 2 pounds)
1 tablespoon salt
1/4 cup peanut oil
black pepper
curry-tomato sauce (following), or
sweet and sour sauce (following)
garnish of:
    slivered preserved ginger
    coriander sprigs

Sprinkle fish with salt and let stand 1 hour.
Wipe off salt with paper toweling and pat dry.
Brown fish in hot oil over medium heat, turning once. If fish is thick, continue cooking 10
to 15 minutes more in 350° oven. Sprinkle
with pepper, pour sauce over and garnish.

CURRY-TOMATO SAUCE

2 tablespoons peanut oil
1 slice ginger root, minced
1 garlic clove, minced
1/2 bell pepper or sweet chili pepper, cut
    in chunks
3 tomatoes, quartered
1 teaspoon curry powder or to taste
binder of:
    2 tablespoons water
    1 tablespoon cornstarch
1/2 teaspoon Oriental sesame oil

Heat oil in a wok or skillet and stir-fry ginger,
garlic and bell or sweet pepper 1 minute. Add
tomatoes and curry powder. Cover and cook
until pepper is just tender, about 2 minutes.
Bind with cornstarch mixture and blend in
sesame oil.

SWEET AND SOUR SAUCE

1 cup cold water
2 tablespoons catsup
2 tablespoons rice vinegar
2 tablespoons cornstarch
2 tablespoons sugar
1-1/2 tablespoons plum sauce or fruit chutney
1 carrot, cut in fine matchstick
1/2 cup matchstick-cut cucumber
1/2 cup thinly sliced onion

Combine ingredients and heat, stirring constantly, until thickened.

STIR-FRIED FISH FILLET WITH BROCCOLI

1/2 pound firm white fish fillet, cut
   into pieces 1/4 inch by 1 inch
1 teaspoon light soy sauce or fish soy
1 teaspoon cornstarch
2 slices ginger root, minced
3 tablespoons peanut oil
1-1/2 pounds Chinese or American broccoli,
   cut in 2-inch lengths
1/2 teaspoon sugar
1/4 cup water
salt to taste
binder of:
   1 teaspoon cornstarch
   1 tablespoon water
1/2 teaspoon Oriental sesame oil

Combine fish with soy, cornstarch and ginger. Heat 2 tablespoons of the peanut oil in a wok or skillet and stir-fry fish mixture gently (so fish does not break apart) until fish just starts to turn white, about 20 seconds. Remove to warm plate. Return wok to heat, add remaining tablespoon of peanut oil and stir-fry broccoli 10 seconds to coat with oil. Add sugar and water, cover and let steam rise to surface. Cook 1 to 2 minutes or until just tender crisp. Return fish to wok, heat through, add salt to taste and bind with cornstarch mixture. Blend in sesame oil.

Note Any vegetable or combination of vegetables (see page 88) may be prepared with fish fillet; the amount of water varies with the vegetable used.

BRAISED FISH WITH FRIED BEAN CURD
Canton

1 pound white fish such as halibut or bass,
   sliced in 1-inch thick fillets
3 tablespoons peanut oil
2 slices ginger root
1 tablespoon chopped Chinese preserved
   turnip (optional)
1 tablespoon brown bean sauce
1 tablespoon light soy sauce
1 tablespoon rice wine or dry sherry
1/2 cup water
2 deep-fried bean-curd cakes (page 58)
binder of:
   1 tablespoon cornstarch
   3 tablespoons water
1/2 teaspoon Oriental sesame oil
salt to taste
3 tablespoons chopped green onion

Pat fish dry. Heat peanut oil in wok or skillet. Brown fish 2 minutes on each side until golden. Combine ginger, turnip, brown bean sauce, soy, wine and stock. Add to fish, cover, lower heat to medium and continue cooking 15 minutes. Add bean curd, heat through and bind with cornstarch mixture. Blend in sesame oil and add salt. Garnish with chopped green onion.

Variation For a spicier touch, add 2 or more dried red chili peppers to hot oil and brown until pungent. Then brown the fish.

POULTRY

PEKING ROAST DUCK (SIMPLIFIED)

1 4- to 5-pound Long Island duckling
2 teaspoons salt
1/2 cup honey or molasses
1 cup boiling water
hoisin sauce or plum sauce
1 bunch green onions, cut into brushes*

Clean duck and remove excess fat. Bring a large pot of water to boil, and dip duck into boiling water for 2 minutes just to scald skin. Water will not return to boil. Remove duck from pot, pat dry and rub cavity with salt. Hang duck in a cool, drafty place for 4 hours to dry. Combine honey with 1 cup boiling water. After the duck has been drying for 2 hours, brush the duck with honey mixture 3 or 4 times during remaining 2 hours to saturate the skin. This will crisp the skin while the duck is roasting. Place duck on rack over a pan containing 2 inches of water. Roast duck 20 minutes in a 450° oven. Lower heat to 300° and continue roasting for 1 hour. Remove duck, slice off skin and cut skin into pieces 1-1/2 inches by 2 inches. Slice meat into bite-size pieces. Reserve bones for soup stock for winter melon soup or congee. Serve skin and duck pieces with steamed buns or Chinese pancakes and hoisin sauce or plum sauce. Garnish with onion brushes.

*Using whites of onion only, cut in 2-inch lengths and then cut lengthwise into thin shreds up to 1/2 inch of end. Crisp in ice water.

CRISPY DUCK
Szechwan

1 Long Island duckling, about 4 pounds
2 teaspoons salt
4 slices ginger root, chopped
4 green onions, cut in 2-inch lengths
1 teaspoon Szechwan peppercorns, crushed
1 tablespoon rice wine or dry sherry
4 whole star anise
3 tablespoons soy sauce
peanut oil for deep-frying
spiced salt (page 118)

Marinate duck in mixture of salt, ginger, onion, peppercorns, wine and star anise 1 hour. Place duck in a shallow heatproof dish and steam over boiling water 1 hour. Remove from steamer and brush duck with soy. Let stand 15 minutes. Deep-fry until golden; drain and let rest 5 minutes. Cut into bite-size pieces and serve with spiced salt.

POULTRY

ROAST DUCK, HOME STYLE
Canton

1 Long Island duckling, about 3 pounds
2 tablespoons light soy sauce
2 tablespoons oyster sauce
1/2 teaspoon five-spice powder
1 piece dried tangerine peel, soaked to
    soften and minced
2 tablespoons rice wine or dry sherry
1 teaspoon sugar
2 teaspoons brown bean sauce
2 green onions
2 coriander sprigs
salt and pepper
mixture of:
    1 tablespoon honey
    2 tablespoons hot water
plum sauce (optional)

Rub duck with mixture of soy sauce, oyster sauce, five-spice powder, tangerine peel, wine, sugar and brown bean sauce. Place onions and coriander in cavity and let stand 3 hours. Sprinkle with salt and pepper, place on rack in roasting pan and roast in a 400° oven 60 to 75 minutes, turning and basting with honey mixture the last 20 minutes. Let rest 10 minutes and cut into bite-size pieces. Serve with plum sauce, if desired.

TEA-SMOKED DUCK
Szechwan

1 Long Island duckling, about 4 pounds
2 tablespoons spiced salt (following)
1 teaspoon saltpeter*
1/2 cup each rice, brown sugar and black
    tea leaves
peel of 1 lemon or orange, cut up

Rub duck inside and out with mixture of spiced salt and saltpeter. Hang duck in a drafty, shady area to dry about 6 hours. In a heavy pot with lid, combine the rice, sugar, tea leaves and fruit peel. Place a rack over this mixture and place duck on rack. Cover and smoke over low heat 10 minutes. Turn duck over and smoke 10 minutes more. Transfer duck to rack in steamer and steam over boiling water 1-1/2 hours. Remove and cut in bite-size pieces.
Variation After steaming, the duck may be deep-fried in peanut oil for a crispy skin.
*Available in drug stores and Oriental markets

SPICED SALT

1/4 cup salt
1/4 cup Szechwan peppercorns, crushed

Place salt and peppercorns in dry skillet. Stirring constantly, heat over medium fire until salt is golden and peppercorns are pungent. Remove from fire; cool. Store in covered jar.

RED-COOKED DUCK
Shanghai

1 Long Island duckling, about 4 to 5 pounds
marinade of:
- 4 green onions
- 3 slices ginger root
- 4 whole cloves
- 3 whole star anise
- 2 tablespoons sugar
- 1 stick cinnamon
- 1 cup soy sauce
- 1-1/2 cups water
- 2 tablespoons rice wine or dry sherry

In a pot large enough to hold duck, combine marinade ingredients. Bring just to boil, add duck, breast side down, cover and return just to boil. Lower heat to simmer and cook 30 minutes. Turn duck over, add giblets and continue cooking another 30 minutes. Remove duck, cool to lukewarm and cut into bite-size pieces. Strain marinade and spoon a little over duck. Refrigerate remaining marinade for future use.

Variation Substitute chicken for the duck.

STEAMED SALT DUCK
Nanking

1 tablespoon Szechwan peppercorns, crushed
5 tablespoons salt
1 Long Island duckling, about 4 pounds
2 green onions
2 tablespoons rice wine or dry sherry

Place peppercorns and salt in dry skillet. Heat over medium heat, stirring constantly, until peppercorns are pungent and salt is a golden color. Rub duck inside and out with spiced salt. Refrigerate overnight. Next day, rinse duck quickly to remove salt. Pat dry and place in shallow heatproof dish. Place green onions in cavity and rub outside of duck with wine. Steam over boiling water 1 hour. Remove pot from heat and let stand, covered, 30 minutes. Remove duck and discard onions. Cut duck into bite-size pieces and pour juices from steaming dish over.

FRIED SQUAB

2 whole squabs, about 1 pound each
1 tablespoon sugar
2 tablespoons soy sauce
1/4 teaspoon five-spice powder
1 piece dried tangerine peel, soaked to
    soften and minced
2 slices ginger root, minced
2 tablespoons rice wine, dry sherry or
    whiskey
peanut oil for deep-frying
shredded lettuce
spiced salt (page 118)

Marinate squabs 1 hour in mixture of sugar, soy, five-spice powder, tangerine peel, ginger root and wine. Deep-fry in hot oil 5 minutes until crisp. Remove and let stand 5 minutes. Cut into bite-size pieces and place on bed of lettuce. Serve with spiced salt.
Roast Squab Variation Instead of deep-frying, roast squab on a rack in a 500° oven for 30 minutes.

MINCED SQUAB AND FRIED RICE-STICK NOODLES
Peking

1 squab (about 12 ounces), boned and minced
1/2 pound pork loin, minced
3 chicken livers, minced
2 tablespoons rendered chicken fat, at
   room temperature
1 egg yolk
1/4 teaspoon pepper
2 tablespoons chopped green onion
1 teaspoon minced ginger root
2 tablespoons peanut oil
1 cup 1/2-inch dice bamboo shoots
1/2 cup 1/2-inch dice water chestnuts
4 dried forest mushrooms, soaked to soften
   and cut in 1/4-inch dice
1 tablespoon rice wine or dry sherry
1 tablespoon soy sauce
1/2 cup basic chicken stock
binder of:
   2 tablespoons water
   1 tablespoon cornstarch
1 teaspoon Oriental sesame oil
4 ounces rice-stick noodles (py mei fun),
   deep-fried (page 73)
lettuce leaves

Combine meats, chicken fat, egg yolk, pepper, onion and ginger root. Heat peanut oil in a wok or skillet and stir-fry meat mixture until meats lose their red color. Add bamboo shoots, water chestnuts, mushrooms, wine, soy and stock. Bring to boil, cover and simmer 10 minutes. Bind with cornstarch mixture and blend in sesame oil. Place fried noodles on platter. Top with meat-vegetable mixture. Surround platter with lettuce leaves for guests to fill.
Note Wild duck, quail, turkey or chicken may be substituted for the squab.

P O U L T R Y

JELLIED CHICKEN
Shanghai

1/2 fryer chicken
3 cups water
2 slices ginger root
1 green onion
1 teaspoon salt
1 tablespoon unflavored gelatin
1 tablespoon rice wine or dry sherry
reserved cold stock
2 ounces Virginia ham, very thinly sliced
1 cup shredded lettuce
coriander sprigs

In saucepan large enough to hold the chicken, combine water, ginger root, onion and salt. Bring to boil, add chicken, cover and bring back to gentle boil. Lower heat and simmer 20 minutes. Remove chicken and let cool, reserving stock. Bone chicken and cut meat with skin intact into 1-inch by 1-1/2-inch pieces. Set aside. Dissolve gelatin in wine and cold stock and then simmer until reduced to 1-1/2 cups. Let cool. Place ham slices in attractive design on bottom of a deep bowl. Arrange chicken pieces, skin side down, on top of ham and carefully pour in stock. Cover and chill until firm. Unmold onto platter of shredded lettuce and garnish with coriander.

WHITE CUT CHICKEN

1 whole fryer chicken
1 teaspoon sugar
1 tablespoon rice wine or dry sherry
2 green onions, chopped
2 slices ginger root
1 teaspoon salt
1 teaspoon Oriental sesame oil
1 cup reserved stock
binder of:
   1 tablespoon cornstarch
   1 tablespoon water
coriander sprigs or slivered green onions

Marinate chicken in mixture of sugar, wine, onions and ginger 30 minutes. Place in saucepan, sprinkle with salt and add cold water just to cover. Cover saucepan, bring to gentle boil and simmer over medium heat 20 minutes. Remove chicken and cool to lukewarm, reserving stock. Cut chicken into bite-size pieces and set aside on serving platter. Bring 1 cup of reserved stock and sesame oil just to boil. Bind with cornstarch mixture and pour over chicken. Garnish with coriander sprigs or green onions.
Variation Place thin slices of Virginia ham between the cut chicken pieces before pouring heated stock over.

122

STEAMED WHOLE CHICKEN
Szechwan

1 fryer chicken
1 teaspoon salt
1 teaspoon Szechwan peppercorns, crushed
2 green onions, chopped
3 slices ginger root, chopped
1 tablespoon rice wine or dry sherry

Rub chicken inside and out with salt and peppercorns. Place in shallow heatproof bowl. Sprinkle with green onions, ginger and wine. Steam over boiling water 45 minutes. Cut chicken into bite-size pieces and pour accumulated juices over.
Variation Prepare chicken as above, placing 3 whole star anise in cavity before steaming. After steaming, combine the star anise with accumulated juices, bring just to boil and bind with a little cornstarch and cold water to thicken. Pour over cut chicken.

DRUNKEN CHICKEN
Shanghai

1 fryer chicken, halved or
2 whole chicken breasts, halved
2 teaspoons salt
1 cup rice wine or dry sherry
2 green onions, cut up
2 slices ginger root, slivered

Rub chicken with salt and let stand 1 hour. Pour off excess liquid and place chicken in heatproof bowl. Pour 1/2 cup of the wine over, top with green onions and ginger, and steam over boiling water 30 minutes. Remove from heat and cool. Pour remaining wine over chicken and refrigerate at least 4 hours or up to 1 week. The longer the chicken marinates, the drunker it becomes. Cut into bite-size pieces.

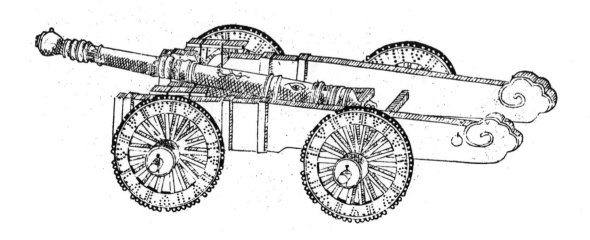

P
O
U
L
T
R
Y

SMOKED CHICKEN
Peking

1 whole fryer chicken
3 tablespoons spiced salt (page 118)
8 cups water
1 green onion
3 slices ginger root
2 whole star anise
1 cinnamon stick
1 cup soy sauce
1/2 cup each brown sugar, rice and black
   tea leaves
1 tablespoon Oriental sesame oil

Rub chicken inside and out with spiced salt. Let stand 4 hours. Combine water, onion, ginger, anise, cinnamon and soy. Bring to boil and simmer 10 minutes. Add chicken; cover and continue cooking 10 more minutes over medium heat. Turn chicken over and cook 5 more minutes. Remove chicken (stock is good for a turnip soup) and set aside. In heavy Dutch oven or wok lined with aluminum foil, combine sugar, rice and tea leaves. Place a rack on top of mixture and lay chicken on its side on rack. Cover and smoke 10 minutes over low heat. Turn chicken over and smoke an additional 10 minutes until browned. Remove chicken and brush with sesame oil. Cut into bite-size pieces and serve.

SALT ROASTED CHICKEN
Peking

This recipe is a good example of the ingenuity of the Chinese. The chicken is roasted on top of the stove. Because it is very important that the chicken be completely dry, some cooks prefer hanging the chicken in a drafty place for an hour before roasting.

1 whole fryer chicken
1 teaspoon five-spice powder
2 slices ginger root
2 green onions, halved
2 coriander sprigs (optional)
4 to 5 pounds coarse salt

Clean and wipe chicken dry inside and out. Rub cavity with five-spice powder and stuff with ginger, green onions and coriander. Stirring frequently, heat the salt in a heavy pot over medium heat at least 30 minutes until salt is very hot. Remove one-third of the hot salt and set aside, leaving at least a 2-inch deep layer of salt in the pot. Place chicken, breast side down, on salt and top with reserved hot salt. Cover pot with tight-fitting lid and cook on lowest heat 1 hour. Remove chicken, brushing off excess salt, and cool to lukewarm. Cut in bite-size pieces. The chicken will be lightly golden, sweet and juicy.

CRISPY CHICKEN
Canton

1 whole fryer chicken
2 tablespoons salt
1 teaspoon five-spice powder
1/4 cup boiling water
1 tablespoon light corn syrup or honey
1 tablespoon rice vinegar
1 tablespoon rice wine or dry sherry
peanut oil for deep-frying
juice of 1 lemon

Dry chicken thoroughly inside and out. Rub salt and five-spice powder into cavity of chicken. Tie legs together with string long enough to hang. Combine boiling water, corn syrup, vinegar and wine and coat outside of chicken well with the mixture. Hang in a cool, drafty place 4 to 6 hours until skin is dry. Pour enough oil to cover chicken in a wok or Dutch oven and heat until very hot. Lower chicken into hot oil; immediately reduce heat so skin does not break, and cook over medium heat 20 minutes, turning frequently so chicken cooks evenly. During the last few minutes of cooking time, raise heat to brown chicken, if necessary. Remove chicken and let it stand 10 minutes. Cut into bite-size pieces, place on heated platter and sprinkle with lemon juice.

RED-COOKED CHICKEN IN SPICES
Szechwan

1 whole fryer chicken
4 cups water
1 teaspoon salt
1/4 cup sugar
1 tablespoon Szechwan peppercorns, crushed
3 whole star anise
1 piece tangerine peel, soaked to soften
1/2 teaspoon five-spice powder
2 slices ginger root
1/4 cup rice wine or dry sherry
1 cup dark soy sauce
1 tablespoon Oriental sesame oil

Rinse chicken, pat dry and set aside. Bring water, salt, sugar, peppercorns, anise, tangerine peel, five-spice powder, ginger root and wine to boil. Add soy sauce and simmer 15 minutes. Add chicken, turn to coat, cover and simmer 10 minutes. Turn chicken over and simmer another 10 minutes. Remove saucepan from heat and let stand, covered, at least 20 minutes. Remove chicken, cool and rub with sesame oil. Reserve cooking liquid. Cut chicken into bite-size pieces and arrange on heated serving platter. Pour 1/4 cup cooking liquid over chicken and serve. Reserve remaining soy liquid for future use; store in covered jar in refrigerator.

VELVET CHICKEN
Canton

1 whole chicken breast, skinned, boned and minced (about 1 cup)
2 teaspoons cornstarch
1/2 teaspoon salt
1/4 cup water
4 egg whites, beaten just until fluffy
3 tablespoons peanut oil
1 cup rich chicken stock
1 teaspoon rice wine or dry sherry
1 tablespoon cornstarch
1/4 cup finely minced Virginia ham

Combine chicken, 2 teaspoons cornstarch and salt. Gradually add water a teaspoonful at a time, mixing well each time. If added too quickly mixture will not hold together. Fold in egg whites. Heat oil over medium heat (do not allow to get too hot) and add chicken mixture. Immediately remove pan from heat, mixing and blending chicken mixture well with the oil. Return to moderate heat and cook 30 to 45 seconds until set and chicken is cooked through. Do not brown. Transfer to heated serving platter and keep warm. Heat stock, wine and 1 tablespoon cornstarch until thickened. Add ham and pour over chicken. Serve immediately.
Velvet Chicken with Peas or Snow Peas Variation Add 1 cup fresh green peas or snow peas to sauce. Cook until just tender.
Velvet Chicken and Shrimp Variation Substitute 1/2 cup raw minced shrimp for half of the chicken.

STEAMED CHICKEN WITH RICE FLOUR
Hupeh

2 whole chicken breasts, boned and cut
   into 1-inch squares
2 slices ginger root, minced
1 tablespoon light soy sauce
1 tablespoon rice wine or dry sherry
1/2 teaspoon salt
1/4 cup rice flour
1/4 teaspoon five-spice powder

Marinate chicken in mixture of ginger, soy and wine 30 minutes. In dry skillet, lightly brown the salt, rice flour and five-spice powder. Cool and combine with chicken, coating well. Place chicken in shallow heatproof dish and steam over boiling water 45 minutes.

CANTONESE FRIED CHICKEN

4 pounds fryer chicken parts
3 tablespoons dark soy sauce
3 garlic cloves, minced
2 slices ginger root, minced
1 teaspoon salt
1/2 teaspoon black pepper
1 egg, beaten
3/4 cup flour
1/4 cup cornstarch
peanut oil for deep-frying

Marinate chicken in mixture of soy, garlic and ginger at least 2 hours. Season with salt and pepper and blend in the beaten egg. Combine flour and cornstarch and sprinkle over chicken pieces to form a thick paste. Heat oil in wok or skillet and fry chicken pieces a few at a time until golden and cooked through. Drain and keep warm in oven until all chicken pieces have been fried.

HOT AND SWEET DICED CHICKEN
Shanghai

1 whole chicken breast, boned and cut
  in 1/2-inch dice
1 egg white
1 teaspoon cornstarch
1/2 teaspoon salt
3 tablespoons peanut oil
2 dried red chili peppers
1 cup diced bamboo shoots
1 cup diced carrots, blanched 1 minute
1/2 cup diced water chestnuts
1 bell pepper, cut in 1/2-inch dice
1 tablespoon hoisin sauce or
  brown bean sauce
2 teaspoons sugar
1 tablespoon rice wine or dry sherry
1 slice ginger root, minced

Combine chicken, egg white, cornstarch and salt. Set aside. Heat peanut oil in wok or skillet and stir-fry chili peppers until pungent and brown. Add chicken mixture and stir-fry 30 seconds. Add vegetables and continue stir-frying another 30 seconds. Blend in remaining ingredients and cook and stir 2 minutes.

PINEAPPLE CHICKEN
Canton

2 whole chicken breasts, boned and cut in
  1-inch chunks
1 tablespoon rice wine or dry sherry
2 teaspoons light soy sauce or hoisin sauce
3 tablespoons peanut oil
3 slices ginger root
1 11-ounce can pineapple chunks, drained,
  juice reserved
1 small onion, cut in 1-inch chunks
1 bell pepper, cut in 1-inch chunks
1 tablespoon sugar
binder of:
  2 tablespoons water
  1 tablespoon cornstarch

Combine chicken, wine and soy. Heat oil in wok or skillet. Add ginger root and stir-fry 30 seconds. Add chicken mixture and stir-fry 1 minute. Measure enough pineapple juice, adding water if needed, to make 1 cup. Add to wok, cover, lower heat to medium and cook for 2 minutes. Add pineapple chunks, onion, bell pepper and sugar. Blend well and cook for 3 minutes. Bind with cornstarch mixture.
Lichee Chicken Variation Substitute 1 cup canned lichees for pineapple.
Sweet and Sour Chicken Variation Add 3 tablespoons rice vinegar and increase sugar to 3 tablespoons when adding reserved juice.

CHICKEN AND PEANUTS WITH CHILI PEPPERS
Szechwan

2 whole chicken breasts
2 slices ginger root, minced
1 teaspoon cornstarch
2 teaspoons light soy sauce
1/2 teaspoon salt
1/4 cup peanut oil
1 cup skinless peanuts
3 to 4 dried red chili peppers
1/2 teaspoon sugar
1 teaspoon rice vinegar

Bone chicken breasts (reserve bones for stock) and dice meat with skin intact. Combine diced chicken with ginger, cornstarch, soy and salt. Set aside. Heat peanut oil in a wok or skillet and stir-fry peanuts 2 minutes. Remove peanuts with slotted spoon, leaving oil in pan, and set aside. Add chili pepper to pan and stir-fry 1 minute until browned and pungent. Remove with slotted spoon, leaving oil in pan, and set aside. Stir-fry chicken 2 minutes. Add sugar, vinegar, reserved peanuts and chilis and heat through. Serve hot.

BRAISED CHICKEN WITH GOLDEN NEEDLES
Canton

1 tablespoon rice wine or dry sherry
2 tablespoons light soy sauce
1/4 teaspoon five-spice powder
1 slice ginger root
1/2 teaspoon Oriental sesame oil
1 fryer chicken, halved, or
2 whole chicken breasts, halved
1/4 cup peanut oil
4 jujubes, soaked to soften and slivered
1/2 cup golden needles, soaked to soften and
    each tied in a knot
3 or 4 dried forest mushrooms, soaked to
    soften and cut in matchstick
1 piece tangerine peel, soaked to soften
    and minced
chicken stock and reserved marinade to
    make 3/4 cup
binder of:
    2 tablespoons water
    1 tablespoon cornstarch
coriander sprigs

Combine wine, 1 tablespoon of the soy sauce, five-spice powder, ginger and sesame oil and marinate chicken in mixture 30 minutes. In a wok or skillet heat peanut oil and brown chicken well, uncovered, about 8 minutes. Add jujubes, golden needles, mushrooms, tangerine peel, remaining soy and stock-marinade mixture. Cover, bring to steam and cook 15 minutes. Remove chicken and cut into bite-size pieces. Bind juices and ingredients in pan with cornstarch mixture; pour over chicken and garnish with coriander sprigs.

BRAISED CHICKEN AND CHESTNUTS
Shanghai

1 fryer chicken, cut up
1/4 cup light soy sauce
peanut oil for deep-frying
1 tablespoon chopped green onion
1 teaspoon chopped ginger root
1 cup dried chestnuts, soaked to soften,
    parboiled 15 minutes, and drained,
    water reserved
1 piece tangerine peel, soaked to soften
    and minced
2 tablespoons rice wine or dry sherry
1 cup reserved chestnut water mixed with:
    1 teaspoon sugar
    1/4 teaspoon black pepper
binder of:
    1 tablespoon water
    1 teaspoon cornstarch
1 teaspoon Oriental sesame oil

Marinate chicken pieces in soy sauce 20 minutes. Drain and reserve soy. Brown chicken in hot oil and drain on paper toweling. Pour off all but 2 tablespoons of oil and stir-fry onion and ginger root 2 minutes. Add chicken, chestnuts, tangerine peel, wine, water mixture and reserved soy. Simmer 15 minutes and bind with cornstarch mixture. Add sesame oil and transfer to heated platter.

CHICKEN AND VEGETABLES

1 whole chicken breast, skinned, boned and
    thinly sliced
1-1/2 teaspoons light soy sauce
1/4 teaspoon Oriental sesame oil
1-1/2 teaspoons rice wine or dry sherry
2 tablespoons peanut oil
1/4 pound snow peas
1/4 cup cloud ears, soaked to soften
1 celery rib, thinly sliced on diagonal
1/2 pound Chinese okra, scraped and cut
    in 1-inch chunks
1/4 cup water
binder of:
    2 tablespoons water
    1 tablespoon cornstarch
2 tablespoons toasted sesame seeds

Marinate chicken in mixture of soy, sesame
oil and wine 10 minutes. Heat 1 tablespoon of
the peanut oil in a wok or skillet and stir-fry
snow peas without browning 1 minute, or
until peas are glossy but undercooked. Remove and set aside. Stir-fry chicken in remaining oil 30 seconds; add cloud ears, celery and
okra and stir-fry 30 more seconds. Add water,
cover, bring to steam and cook 2 to 3 minutes. Return snow peas to wok and bind with
cornstarch mixture. Transfer to heated platter
and sprinkle with sesame seeds.

EIGHT-FLAVORED SHREDDED CHICKEN
Szechwan

2 whole chicken breasts
1 teaspoon Oriental sesame oil
1 teaspoon salt
2 tablespoons peanut oil
3 or more dried red chili peppers, crushed
1 green onion, minced
4 slices ginger root, minced
1 tablespoon sesame-seed paste or peanut
    butter
1 tablespoon each rice vinegar and light
    soy sauce
1 teaspoon sugar
coriander sprigs

Rub chicken breasts with sesame oil and salt.
Place breasts in heatproof dish and steam over
boiling water 20 minutes. Remove from heat
and cool to lukewarm. Bone breasts (save skin
and bones for soup stock) and with fingers
shred meat into thin strips. Set aside. Heat
peanut oil in a wok or skillet. Combine remaining ingredients, except coriander, and
add to hot oil; stir well and immediately remove from heat. Pour over chicken and garnish with coriander.
Variation Place chicken on bed of shredded
iceberg lettuce or sliced cucumbers.

BRAISED CHICKEN WITH OYSTER SAUCE
Canton

3 tablespoons peanut oil
3 slices ginger root
1 fryer chicken, cut into bite-size pieces, or
2 whole chicken breasts, cut into bite-size
    pieces
1/4 cup oyster sauce
1/2 cup hot water
2 tablespoons rice wine or dry sherry
1 teaspoon sugar
1 bell pepper, cut in chunks
binder of:
    1 tablespoon water
    1 teaspoon cornstarch
2 green onions, cut in 1-inch lengths

Heat oil in wok or skillet and stir-fry ginger root 10 seconds. Add chicken pieces and stir-fry until chicken is golden brown on all sides. Blend in oyster sauce, water, wine and sugar. Cover, lower heat and simmer 20 minutes. Add bell pepper and cook 5 minutes. Bind with cornstarch mixture and garnish with green onions.

CHICKEN WITH DRIED FOREST MUSHROOMS

1/2 fryer chicken, cut in bite-size pieces
6 to 8 dried forest mushrooms, soaked to
    soften and halved or quartered
6 cups water
1 tablespoon rice wine or dry sherry
1 teaspoon salt
2 green onions, cut in 1-inch pieces
2 slices ginger root, chopped
1 dried tangerine peel, soaked to soften

Combine all ingredients in heatproof earthen pot. Bring to boil, cover, lower heat and simmer 1 hour.
Variation One large squab or 1/2 duck may be substituted for the chicken.

CHICKEN WITH NUTS AND VEGETABLES

3 tablespoons peanut oil
1-1/2 cups raw cashews, blanched almonds or walnuts
1 whole chicken breast, skinned, boned and thinly sliced
1 teaspoon hoisin sauce
1 tablespoon rice wine or dry sherry
1/4 pound snow peas
1 bell pepper, cut in 1-inch chunks
1/4 cup water
binder of:
    2 tablespoons water
    1 tablespoon cornstarch
1/2 cup slivered green onions

Heat peanut oil in a wok or skillet and, over low heat, stirring constantly, fry nuts until golden. Remove nuts with slotted spoon and set aside, leaving oil in pan. Combine chicken, hoisin sauce and wine. Stir-fry in oil 1 minute. Add snow peas, reserved nuts, bell pepper and water. Cover, let steam rise and cook 2 minutes. Bind with cornstarch mixture and transfer to heated platter. Sprinkle with onions.

SWEET AND SOUR CHICKEN WINGS
Shanghai

2 pounds chicken wings, tips removed
    (reserve for soup stock)
2 tablespoons soy sauce
2 slices ginger root, minced
2 green onions, chopped
1/2 teaspoon minced garlic
1 tablespoon rice wine or dry sherry
1 egg, beaten
1/2 cup unbleached flour
peanut oil for deep-frying
shredded iceberg lettuce
sweet and sour sauce (page 114)
1/4 cup toasted sesame seeds

Marinate chicken wings in mixture of soy, ginger, green onions, garlic and wine 3 hours. Place in bowl, pour beaten egg over and mix well. Add flour and stir to coat wings well. Fry wings in hot oil, 1/2-inch deep, in one layer until golden; drain on paper toweling as wings are fried. Place on bed of shredded lettuce and pour sweet and sour sauce over. Sprinkle with sesame seeds and serve hot.

CHICKEN LIVERS AND CUCUMBERS
Kiangsu

3 tablespoons peanut oil
2 green onions, cut in 1-1/2-inch pieces
1/2 pound chicken livers, sliced 1/4 inch thick
3/4 pound small cucumbers, halved length-
    wise and sliced thickly on diagonal
2 tablespoons dried shrimp, soaked to soften
    in 1/4 cup warm water, water reserved
1 teaspoon rice wine or dry sherry
1/2 teaspoon each salt and sugar
1 teaspoon light soy sauce
binder of:
    1 tablespoon water
    1 teaspoon cornstarch

Heat oil in a skillet or wok and stir-fry onions 10 seconds; add chicken livers and stir-fry, stirring constantly, another 30 seconds. Add cucumbers, dried shrimp, wine, salt, sugar and soy. Stir and cook 10 seconds and add shrimp water. Cover and cook 2 minutes until steam rises to surface. Bind with cornstarch mixture and serve immediately.

FRIED GIZZARDS AND LIVERS
Canton

6 chicken gizzards
6 chicken livers
1 teaspoon minced ginger root
1 tablespoon rice wine or dry sherry
1 tablespoon soy sauce
1 egg, beaten
1/4 cup each flour and cornstarch, combined
peanut oil for deep-frying
chili oil
soy sauce

Cut gizzards in half, removing center tough membrane; slash in crisscross pattern, but do not cut through. Halve livers and combine with gizzards, ginger root, wine and soy. Let stand 30 minutes. Mix in egg, sprinkle with flour-cornstarch mixture and blend just enough to coat lightly. Deep-fry in hot oil and serve with chili oil and soy sauce.

MEATS

BASIC STEAMED PORK
Canton

1 pound ground or thinly sliced pork butt
2 tablespoons water
1 tablespoon cornstarch
1 tablespoon soy sauce
1 teaspoon peanut oil
1 teaspoon rice wine or dry sherry
1/2 teaspoon salt
1/2 cup minced water chestnuts (optional)

Combine all ingredients in a shallow heat-proof dish. Spread mixture to within 1/2 inch of rim of dish, keeping center slightly indented. Steam over boiling water 25 minutes. Skim excess fat from surface of meat and serve hot with freshly cooked rice.

Variation with Ham or Chinese Sausage Reduce salt in basic steamed pork to 1/4 teaspoon. Add 1/4 pound ham or Chinese sausage, finely minced.

Variation with Forest Mushrooms Before steaming, arrange on top of meat mixture 3 dried forest mushrooms, soaked to soften and cut in thin slivers.

Variation with Chinese Preserved Turnips Omit salt in basic steamed pork or steamed pork with ham or Chinese sausage. Before steaming, arrange on top of meat 2 tablespoons chopped Chinese preserved turnips, well rinsed.

Variation with Tea Melon Spread 6 tea melons, thinly sliced, evenly on top of meat before steaming.

Variation with Salted Fish Omit salt in basic steamed pork. Arrange on top of meat before steaming, 2 to 4 1-inch by 2-inch pieces salt fish and 2 slices ginger root, cut in fine slivers. Drizzle 1 teaspoon peanut oil over fish pieces.

Variation with Preserved Szechwan Cabbage Omit salt in basic steamed pork. Arrange on top before steaming 1/4 cup thinly sliced preserved Szechwan cabbage.

Variation with Salted Bamboo Shoots Omit salt in basic steamed pork. Arrange on top before steaming, 1/3 cup salted bamboo shoots, well rinsed.

Variation with Fermented Bean Cake or Red Bean-Curd Cheese Omit salt in basic steamed pork. Combine 2 tablespoons of fermented bean cake or red bean-curd cheese, mashed, with the meat mixture before steaming.

137

MEATS

BRAISED STUFFED MUSHROOMS
Canton

18 medium dried forest mushrooms, soaked
   to soften, stems removed
cornstarch for dusting
1/2 pound ground pork butt
1/4 pound raw shrimp, shelled and minced
1/2 cup minced water chestnuts
1/4 cup minced smoked ham
1 tablespoon cornstarch
1 tablespoon light soy sauce
1 teaspoon rice wine or dry sherry
1 small piece dried tangerine peel, soaked to
   soften and minced
1/4 cup peanut oil
3/4 cup chicken stock
binder of:
   1 tablespoon water
   1 teaspoon cornstarch
1/2 teaspoon Oriental sesame oil

Pat mushrooms dry. Dust stem side with cornstarch and set aside. Combine pork, shrimp, water chestnuts, ham, cornstarch, soy, wine and tangerine peel. Fill each mushroom with about 1 tablespoon of mixture, patting in firmly. In heavy skillet heat peanut oil and brown mushrooms, meat side down. Turn over and add stock. Cover and simmer 20 minutes. Remove mushrooms to heated platter. Bind juices with cornstarch mixture and add sesame oil. Pour over mushrooms and serve immediately.

Steamed Stuffed Mushrooms Variation Omit chicken stock and binder. Mix sesame oil in with meat mixture. Place filled mushrooms meat side up in heatproof dish. Steam above boiling water 40 minutes.

Braised Stuffed Bell Pepper or Bitter Melon Variation Using either 3 bell peppers or 2 bitter melons instead of the mushrooms, cut into quarters lengthwise and then in half again crosswise. Remove seeds. Fill and follow directions for stuffed mushrooms.

PORK BALLS AND CABBAGE
Shanghai

1 tablespoon peanut oil
2 pounds Napa cabbage, cut in 2-inch pieces
1 pound lean ground pork butt
1 teaspoon salt
1 teaspoon Oriental sesame oil
1 teaspoon rice wine or dry sherry
1 piece tangerine peel, soaked to soften
   and minced
1/2 teaspoon black pepper
1 tablespoon chopped green onion
1/2 teaspoon minced ginger root
1 tablespoon cornstarch
peanut oil for browning
1 cup stock
1 tablespoon light soy sauce

Heat peanut oil in a wok or skillet and stir-fry cabbage just to wilt. Line a heatproof earthen pot with cabbage and set aside. Combine pork, salt, sesame oil, wine, tangerine peel, pepper, onion and ginger root. Form into 4 balls and coat them with cornstarch. Brown on all sides in oil and arrange on top of cabbage. Combine stock and soy and pour over. Bring just to boil, cover, lower heat and simmer 40 minutes.

MEATS

STIR-FRIED PORK WITH ASPARAGUS

1/2 pound lean boneless pork butt, sliced thinly
2 teaspoons light soy sauce or oyster sauce
1 teaspoon rice wine or dry sherry
1 teaspoon cornstarch
1 slice ginger root, minced (optional)
1 garlic clove, minced (optional)
3 tablespoons peanut oil
1-1/2 pounds asparagus, sliced diagonally 1/2 inch thick
1/2 teaspoon sugar
1/4 cup water
salt to taste
binder of:
    1 teaspoon cornstarch
    1 tablespoon water
1/2 teaspoon Oriental sesame oil

Combine pork, soy, wine, cornstarch, ginger and garlic. Heat 2 tablespoons of the peanut oil in wok or skillet. Stir-fry pork mixture until meat loses its pinkness, about 1-1/2 minutes. Remove to warm plate. Return wok to heat, add remaining tablespoon of peanut oil and stir-fry asparagus 10 seconds to coat with oil. Add sugar and water. Cover, let steam rise to surface and cook until asparagus is just tender crisp, about 2 minutes. Return pork to wok, heat through, add salt to taste and bind with cornstarch mixture. Blend in sesame oil. *Szechwan Variation* Increase sugar to 1 teaspoon and add 2 teaspoons rice vinegar and chili oil to taste with the water.
Note Any vegetable or combination of vegetables (see page 88) may be prepared with pork; the amount of water varies with the vegetable used.

SWEET AND SOUR PORK

1-1/2 pounds boneless lean pork butt, cut
   in 1-inch cubes
2 tablespoons sugar
1 teaspoon salt
1/2 teaspoon five-spice powder
2 tablespoons hoisin sauce
1 tablespoon rice wine or dry sherry
fruit sweet and sour sauce (following)
1 tablespoon toasted sesame seeds

Combine meat with sugar, salt and five-spice
powder. Coat well with hoisin sauce and wine
and marinate 2 to 4 hours. Bake in 400° oven
40 minutes. Drain off any fat and add pork to
sweet and sour sauce. Reheat and sprinkle
with sesame seeds.

FRUIT SWEET AND SOUR SAUCE

1 cup canned pineapple chunks
1 cup canned longans or lichees
1/4 cup rice wine vinegar
1 tablespoon catsup
2 tablespoons sugar
1 tablespoon cornstarch
1 bell pepper, seeded and cut up
1/2 onion, cut into eighths

Drain fruits and measure juice to make 1 cup,
adding water if needed. Set fruits aside and
combine juice with vinegar, catsup, sugar and
cornstarch. Cook and stir over medium heat
until thickened and clear. Add fruits, green
pepper and onion and bring just to boil.

MEATS

BARBECUED PORK
(CHA SIEW)
Canton

Make enough barbecued pork to have on hand to use in all sorts of recipes such as stir-fried vegetables and noodle dishes.

1 3-pound piece lean boneless pork butt
1/3 cup hoisin sauce
1/3 cup sugar
2 tablespoons rice wine or gin
2 tablespoons oyster sauce
1/2 teaspoon five-spice powder
1/2 teaspoon saltpeter (optional)*

Cut pork with the grain into long strips 1-1/2 inches square. Combine remaining ingredients and marinate pork strips at least 4 hours. Place in single layer on rack in roasting pan. Bake in preheated 375° oven 45 minutes or until done, basting and turning every 15 minutes. If cooking over charcoal, cook on high rack and watch carefully. Turn frequently. To serve, slice thinly.

*Available in Oriental markets and drug stores. Gives pork the red color.

CRISPY SKIN ROAST PORK

1 5-pound whole boneless pork butt with skin
1/4 cup brown bean sauce
1 teaspoon five-spice powder
1 teaspoon Szechwan peppercorns, crushed
1 teaspoon salt
2 tablespoons honey, dissolved in
1/2 cup hot water

Scald pork by dipping into boiling water for 1 minute. Remove and hang in a cool, drafty place for 2 hours to tighten skin. Cut the pork butt halfway through so that all of the skin is exposed on one side. Spread flat, skin side down, on cutting board and make long slashes 1/2 inch deep, being careful not to cut too deeply. Combine brown bean sauce, five-spice powder, peppercorns and salt. Rub mixture on meat side only and let stand 2 hours. Place on rack in roasting pan skin side up. Roast in preheated 400° oven 15 minutes. Lower heat to 325° and continue roasting 1-1/2 to 2 hours or until done, brushing with honey-water mixture the last 15 minutes. Cut meat into bite-size pieces so each piece has some crispy skin.

TWICE-COOKED PORK
Peking

1 1-1/2-pound piece boneless pork butt
2 tablespoons rice wine or dry sherry
1 green onion, halved
2 slices ginger root
1-1/2 cups water
3 tablespoons peanut oil
1 green bell pepper, cut in 1-inch chunks
1 red bell pepper, cut in 1-inch chunks
2 garlic cloves, thinly sliced
2 tablespoons hoisin sauce
1 tablespoon hot bean paste
2 tablespoons soy sauce
2 teaspoons sugar

Combine pork, wine, green onion, ginger and water. Bring just to boil, cover, lower heat and simmer 20 minutes. Remove meat and slice with the grain in thin slices. (Strain and reserve liquid for soup stock.) Heat oil in a wok or skillet and stir-fry pork slices 1 minute. Add peppers and garlic and stir-fry another minute. Combine remaining ingredients and add to pan; blend well and cook 1 minute.

PORK WITH MINCED GARLIC
Szechwan

1 1-pound piece boneless lean pork butt
2 green onions
2 slices ginger root
1-1/2 cups water
2 tablespoons peanut oil
3 garlic cloves, minced
1 teaspoon each salt and sugar
1 tablespoon rice vinegar
1 tablespoon soy sauce
1 teaspoon chili oil

Combine pork, green onions, ginger root and water. Bring just to boil, lower heat and simmer 30 minutes. Remove pork and slice thinly with the grain. (Strain liquid and reserve for stock.) Arrange pork slices on heated platter. Heat peanut oil in wok or skillet and stir-fry garlic 1 minute; remove skillet from heat and mix in remaining ingredients. Pour over pork slices and serve warm or at room temperature.

MEATS

BARBECUED SPARERIBS
Canton

3 pounds lean pork spareribs
1/4 cup each hoisin sauce and sugar
1 tablespoon rice wine or dry sherry
1 tablespoon oyster sauce
1/2 teaspoon five-spice powder
1/2 teaspoon saltpeter (optional)*

Cut spareribs in half lengthwise and crack ends. Keep in 2 pieces. Rub with mixture of remaining ingredients and marinate at least 4 hours. Place in single layer on rack in roasting pan. Cook, turning and basting, in a preheated 400° oven 10 minutes. Lower heat to 375° and continue cooking, turning occasionally and basting for 1 hour. If cooking over charcoal, cook on high rack and watch carefully. Turn occasionally.
*Available in drug stores and Oriental markets

STEAMED SPARERIBS WITH FERMENTED BEAN CAKE
Canton

1-1/2 pounds pork spareribs, cut in
    1-inch pieces
2 tablespoons fermented bean cake or
    red bean-curd cheese
1 tablespoon liquid from fermented bean
    cake or red bean-curd cheese
1 tablespoon cornstarch
1/2 teaspoon sugar
1/2 teaspoon Oriental sesame oil

Combine all ingredients in shallow heatproof dish and steam over boiling water 40 minutes.

STEAMED SPARERIBS WITH THREE SAUCES

1-1/2 pounds pork spareribs, cut in
    1-inch pieces
1 tablespoon brown bean sauce
1 tablespoon oyster sauce
1 tablespoon soy sauce
1 tablespoon rice wine or dry sherry
1 tablespoon cornstarch
1 teaspoon peanut oil

Combine all ingredients in shallow heatproof dish and steam over boiling water 40 minutes.

PORK KIDNEY, CUCUMBER AND MUNG BEAN SPROUTS
Hunan

3 pork kidneys, about 1 pound
1 slice ginger root
1 teaspoon salt
1/2 pound mung bean sprouts, blanched
   30 seconds and drained
1/2 pound small cucumbers
1 teaspoon salt
2 ripe tomatoes, sliced
sauce of:
   2 tablespoons light soy sauce
   1/2 teaspoon each salt and sugar
   1 tablespoon rice vinegar
   1 teaspoon Oriental sesame oil
   1/4 teaspoon black pepper
   1/2 teaspoon chili oil

Split kidneys lengthwise, remove white veins
and slice diagonally into 1/8-inch thick slices.
Soak in cold water to cover 1 hour. Drain and
boil 4 minutes in water with ginger root and 1
teaspoon salt. Drain, rinse in cold water and
drain again. Set aside. Score cucumbers and
slice thinly. Sprinkle with 1 teaspoon salt and
let stand 10 minutes. Squeeze out excess
water and set aside. Place bean sprouts in
center of plate and top with kidney slices.
Surround with cucumber and tomato. Combine sauce ingredients and pour over all. Serve
as first course.

CURRIED LAMB STEW
Canton

3 tablespoons peanut oil
2 slices ginger root, minced
2 garlic cloves, minced
2 pounds lamb stew, cut in 1-inch pieces
1 tablespoon soy sauce
1 tablespoon rice wine or dry sherry
1 to 2 tablespoons curry powder
1-1/2 cups water
3 carrots, cut in chunks
1 onion, cut in chunks
2 celery ribs, cut in chunks
2 potatoes, cut in chunks
1 bell pepper, cut in chunks
binder of:
    2 tablespoons water
    1 tablespoon cornstarch
salt and pepper
coriander sprigs

Heat oil in a skillet or wok and stir-fry ginger and garlic 10 seconds; add meat and stir-fry 5 minutes to brown on all sides. Add soy, wine, curry powder and water. Bring to boil, cover, lower heat and simmer 1 hour. Add carrots, onion, celery and potatoes. Continue cooking 20 minutes. Add bell pepper and cook an additional 5 minutes. Bind with cornstarch mixture, season to taste with salt and pepper and garnish with coriander sprigs.

SHREDDED LAMB WITH BEAN-THREAD NOODLES
Peking

1 pound lean lamb, cut in shreds
1 tablespoon light soy sauce
2 teaspoons rice wine or dry sherry
3 tablespoons peanut oil
1 onion, cut in shreds
1 cup matchstick-cut bamboo shoots
1/2 cup matchstick-cut water chestnuts
3 dried forest mushrooms, soaked to soften
    and cut in shreds
1/4 pound snow peas or green beans,
    cut in shreds
1/2 cup hot water
binder of:
    2 tablespoons water
    1 tablespoon cornstarch
2 ounces bean-thread noodles, deep fried
    (page 73)

Combine lamb, soy and wine. Heat peanut oil in a wok or skillet and stir-fry lamb with onions 30 seconds. Add bamboo shoots, water chestnuts and mushrooms. Stir-fry 1 more minute. Add snow peas and hot water. Cook, stirring constantly, 1 minute or until peas are tender crisp. Bind with cornstarch mixture. Make a bed of half of the noodles on a heated platter. Top with meat mixture and sprinkle remaining noodles over.

MONGOLIAN GRILL
Peking

A favorite do-it-yourself winter meal to warm the palate and the hands. The sauce is mixed by each guest from the choice of condiments which are placed in small dishes. The unseasoned lamb is cooked over a charcoal fire on a mesh grill by each guest, dipped in beaten egg, and then in sauce. Steamed buns (page 161) are a perfect accompaniment. Serve with any pickled vegetable.

1/4 to 1/3 pound boneless lamb per person, thinly sliced
1 egg per person, slightly beaten (in individual bowls)
condiments:
    soy sauce
    sesame-seed paste or peanut butter
    hoisin sauce
    chili oil
    Oriental sesame oil
    minced garlic
    minced green onions
    sugar
    water or brewed tea for diluting sauce

Variation Mix a sauce from choice of condiments and each guest dips meat into sauce before grilling. Proceed as above. A good combination, which is enough for 4 individual serving bowls, is:
1/2 cup soy sauce
1 cup brewed tea, at room temperature
1 tablespoon sugar
3 garlic cloves, minced
1/2 cup minced green onions
1/4 cup minced coriander leaves

MONGOLIAN LAMB

1-1/2 pounds lamb from leg, cut into 1-inch cubes
2 tablespoons hoisin sauce
1 teaspoon cornstarch
1/2 teaspoon chili oil (optional)
2 tablespoons peanut oil
2 garlic cloves, minced
2 slices ginger root, minced
1 Spanish onion, cut in chunks

Coat lamb with mixture of hoisin sauce, cornstarch and chili oil. Heat peanut oil in a wok or skillet and stir-fry lamb with remaining ingredients 2 minutes. Do not overcook; lamb is best when cooked medium rare.
Variation Beef steak may be substituted for the lamb.

BARBECUED LAMB
Shanghai

3 pounds boned leg of lamb, cut in 1-1/2-inch
  cubes
marinade of:
   2 tablespoons light soy sauce
   2 tablespoons hoisin sauce
   2 tablespoons rice wine or dry sherry
   1/2 teaspoon five-spice powder
   1 tablespoon sugar
   3 slices ginger root, minced
   2 green onions, chopped
   1 teaspoon Oriental sesame oil

Combine marinade ingredients and marinate
lamb 1 hour. Thread lamb on bamboo skew-
ers and broil over hot coals, turning and basting with marinade frequently, for approximately 7 minutes. Do not overcook; lamb
should be pink and juicy.
Note Leg of lamb may be boned and kept in
1 piece. Marinate as above and barbecue 20 to
30 minutes, turning and basting often.

BEEF OR LAMB AND TURNIPS IN EARTHEN POT
Hunan

1 pound beef or lamb stew meat, cut in
  1-inch cubes
1 tablespoon soy sauce
1 teaspoon cornstarch
3 tablespoons peanut oil
2 thin slices ginger root
3 whole star anise
1/2 teaspoon fennel seeds
1 piece tangerine peel, soaked to soften
1-1/2 pounds Chinese turnips or daikon,
  cut in chunks
2 leeks, cut in 2-inch lengths
6 cups beef stock or water
1 teaspoon salt
1 teaspoon Szechwan peppercorns, crushed

Combine meat with soy and cornstarch.
Brown on all sides in oil and transfer to heatproof earthen pot. Add remaining ingredients,
bring just to boil, cover, lower heat and simmer 2 hours.

MEATS

BASIC STEAMED BEEF
Canton

1 pound flank steak, sliced thinly on
    diagonal, or
1 pound lean ground beef
2 teaspoons cornstarch
2 teaspoons rice wine or dry sherry
1 tablespoon each soy sauce and water
1 teaspoon peanut oil
1/2 teaspoon salt
1 slice ginger root, finely minced
1/2 cup minced water chestnuts (optional)

Combine all ingredients and place in shallow, heatproof dish, flattening meat out smoothly to 1/2 inch from rim of bowl, leaving an indentation in center. Place bowl on rack and steam above boiling water 20 minutes.

Variation with Preserved Szechwan Cabbage Omit salt. Place 1/2 cup thinly sliced Szechwan cabbage on top of meat before steaming.

Variation with Salted Bamboo Shoots Omit salt. Place 1/2 cup well-rinsed salted bamboo shoots on top of meat before steaming.

Variation with Chinese Preserved Turnip Place 2 tablespoons well-rinsed Chinese preserved turnip, chopped, on top of meat before steaming.

Variation with Tea Melon Place 1/2 cup slivered tea melon on meat before steaming.

STEAMED BEEF WITH RICE CRUMBS
Szechwan

1 pound flank or skirt steak, cut in
    1-inch squares
1 tablespoon soy sauce
1 tablespoon brown bean sauce
1 tablespoon rice wine or dry sherry
3 tablespoons water
1 teaspoon sugar
1 teaspoon Oriental sesame oil
1 slice ginger root, minced
1/3 cup rice crumbs, following

Marinate beef in all ingredients except rice crumbs 30 minutes. Coat each piece of meat well with rice crumbs and place in shallow heatproof dish, pouring any leftover marinade over. Steam over boiling water 1 hour until rice crumbs are tender. Be careful water does not evaporate during steaming. Add boiling water as needed.

RICE CRUMBS

1 cup long-grain rice
1 teaspoon Szechwan peppercorns
1 whole star anise

In a dry skillet, combine rice, peppercorns and star anise. Over low heat, stir mixture until the rice grains are lightly toasted, about 5 to 7 minutes. Remove skillet from heat and allow rice mixture to cool. Place in blender and blend to the consistency of bread crumbs. Store in a covered jar.

STIR-FRIED BEEF WITH
BOK CHOY (CHINESE CHARD)

1/2 pound flank steak, sliced thinly
   on diagonal
1 tablespoon soy sauce or oyster sauce
2 teaspoons rice wine or dry sherry
1 teaspoon cornstarch
1 slice ginger root, minced
1 garlic clove, minced
3 tablespoons peanut oil
1-1/2 pounds bok choy (Chinese chard), cut
   in 2-inch lengths
1/2 teaspoon sugar
salt to taste
binder of:
   1 teaspoon cornstarch
   1 tablespoon water
1/2 teaspoon Oriental sesame oil

Combine beef, soy, wine, cornstarch, ginger
and garlic. Heat 2 tablespoons of the peanut
oil in a wok or skillet and stir-fry meat mixture 1 minute until meat loses its redness.
Remove to warm plate. Return wok to heat,
add remaining tablespoon of peanut oil and
stir-fry bok choy 10 seconds to coat with oil.
Add sugar, cover and let steam rise to surface.
Cook 1 to 2 minutes or until just tender crisp.
Return beef to pan, heat through, add salt to
taste and bind with cornstarch mixture. Blend
in sesame oil.
Note Any vegetable or combination of vegetables (see page 88) may be prepared with
beef; the amount of water varies with the
vegetable used.

MEATS

151

MEATS

SHREDDED BEEF AND ONIONS
Shanghai

3/4 pound lean beef steak, cut across grain
    into fine shreds
1 tablespoon dark soy sauce
1 tablespoon cornstarch
1 teaspoon sugar
5 tablespoons peanut oil
2 onions, thinly sliced
2 slices ginger root, finely shredded
1/2 teaspoon salt
2 teaspoons light soy sauce
3/4 cup water

Combine beef, dark soy, cornstarch, sugar and 1 tablespoon of the oil. Set aside. Heat 2 tablespoons of the oil in a wok or skillet and stir-fry onions and ginger with the salt and light soy 1 minute. Add water, cover and cook 5 minutes. Transfer to a heated platter. Return skillet to high heat and add remaining 2 tablespoons oil. Stir-fry marinated beef shreds quickly. Return onion mixture to skillet, stir well and heat through.

STIR-FRIED GINGER BEEF
Canton

1 pound flank or skirt steak, sliced thinly
    on diagonal
1 tablespoon dark soy sauce
1/2 teaspoon salt
2 teaspoons rice wine or dry sherry
3 tablespoons peanut oil
1/2 cup very thinly sliced young ginger
    root*, or
4 slices ginger root, slivered
1/2 cup hot beef stock or water
binder of:
    2 tablespoons water
    1 tablespoon cornstarch
coriander sprigs

Combine steak, soy, salt and wine. Set aside. Heat oil in a wok or skillet and stir-fry ginger 10 seconds; remove with slotted spoon and set aside. Return skillet to heat and stir-fry meat mixture 30 seconds. Return ginger to skillet with stock, bind with cornstarch mixture and serve immediately garnished with coriander.

*Young shoots of ginger, light, tender, sweet and pungent; available in spring and summer months.

STEAK KEW
Canton

1 pound flank, skirt steak or other tender
   beef, cut in 1-inch squares
1 onion, cut in 1-inch chunks
1 tablespoon oyster sauce
1 tablespoon soy sauce
1/4 teaspoon pepper
1 teaspoon cornstarch
1 or 2 garlic cloves, minced
1 or 2 slices ginger root, minced
1/2 pound snow peas, or
1 pound Chinese or regular broccoli or
   fresh asparagus tips, or
1 pound firm ripe tomatoes, cut in wedges
3 tablespoons peanut oil

Combine beef, onion, oyster sauce, soy, pepper, cornstarch, garlic and ginger. Let stand 15 minutes. Blanch snow peas, broccoli or asparagus 1 to 2 minutes; drain and place on heated platter; keep warm. If using tomatoes, have at room temperature. Heat peanut oil in a wok or skillet and stir-fry meat and onion mixture 1 to 2 minutes; meat should be well seared but still pink inside. Immediately pour over blanched vegetable and serve. Or place on heated platter and surround with tomato wedges.

Variation with Hoisin Sauce Omit oyster sauce and add 1-1/2 tablespoons hoisin sauce and 1/2 teaspoon Oriental sesame oil.

Variation with Hot Bean Paste Omit oyster sauce and add 2 teaspoons hot bean paste and 1/2 teaspoon Oriental sesame oil.

SPICED BEEF
Szechwan

1 pound beef round steak, cut in shreds or
   ground once
1/4 cup soy sauce
1 tablespoon rice wine or dry sherry
1 teaspoon sugar
1 teaspoon minced ginger root
6 tablespoons peanut oil
3 or more dried red chili peppers
1 carrot, cut in matchstick
2 celery ribs, cut in matchstick
1/2 teaspoon Oriental sesame oil

Marinate beef in mixture of soy, wine, sugar and ginger 30 minutes. Heat 3 tablespoons of the peanut oil in a wok or skillet and stir-fry peppers 30 seconds. Add carrots, stir-fry 30 seconds and add celery. Stir-fry 1 minute and remove to plate. Return skillet to heat and stir-fry beef in remaining peanut oil over high heat until well browned. Return vegetables to skillet and heat through. Blend in sesame oil.

SZECHWAN BEEF STEW

2 pounds beef stew meat, cut in 1-1/2-inch
   chunks
4 green onions, halved lengthwise
4 slices ginger root
3 whole star anise
1/3 cup peanut oil
4 garlic cloves, bruised
1 teaspoon Szechwan peppercorns, crushed
1 tablespoon hot bean paste
1/2 cup soy sauce
2 tablespoons rice wine or dry sherry
1 teaspoon each salt and sugar

Place meat, green onions, ginger and star anise in saucepan and cover with boiling water 2 inches above surface of meat. Cover and simmer 1 hour. Heat peanut oil in a wok or skillet and stir-fry garlic and peppercorns 1 minute or until pungent. Add hot bean paste, soy, wine, salt and sugar. Bring to boil and cook 2 minutes. Strain this mixture into stew and continue cooking 1 hour or until meat is tender. This dish is excellent over boiled fresh noodles.

Note Brown bean sauce may be substituted for the hot bean paste.

RED-COOKED BEEF TONGUE
Shanghai

1 4-pound beef tongue
1 recipe marinade for red-cooked duck
  (page 119)

Parboil tongue in boiling water to cover 10 minutes. Discard water and remove tough white skin from tongue. Simmer tongue in marinade for 2 to 3 hours or until tender, turning once at midpoint of cooking time. Slice and arrange on heated platter. Strain 1/2 cup of the hot marinade and pour over slices.

FIREPOT COOKING

The firepot was first introduced to China when the Mongols invaded the country during the 13th century. The traditional firepot is made of shiny brass and has a chimney and charcoal brazier built in so that red hot coals may be used for keeping the broth at a simmer. It is not necessary, however, to have this kind of pot to do firepot cooking. A deep electric skillet or casserole cooker, or a kettle over a brazier or hot plate may be used. The broth is first prepared on the stove. Bring the water or stock, ginger root and green onions to a boil and boil 15 minutes. Discard the ginger root and onions and pour the broth into the firepot at the table. Place platters of attractively arranged foods near the pot, along with containers of various condiments from which diners may choose for mixing their own sauces. Provide each diner with a small wire strainer (available in Oriental stores) for holding the foods while cooking them, or if these can not be purchased, chopsticks may be used to grasp the meats and vegetables while they are cooking. Also needed are small dishes for mixing dipping sauces, a small bowl containing beaten egg, soup bowls and porcelain soup spoons. Each person selects foods from the platter, cooks them in the broth to desired doneness and then with chopsticks, dips the hot cooked morsels first into the beaten egg to cool and coat them slightly and then into the dipping sauce. Meats and seafoods are generally eaten first, then the vegetables. While the individual cooking is going on, the broth is acquiring all kinds of interesting flavors from the various cooked ingredients. When the last morsel is cooked, add the bean-thread noodles to the broth and simmer just until tender. Finish the meal with the broth and noodles.

MANY TREASURES FIREPOT

for broth:
    4 quarts clear chicken or pork stock,
        or water
    2 slices ginger root
    2 green onions
platters of:
    1 whole chicken breast, slivered
    1/2 pound lean pork butt, thinly sliced
    1/2 pound tender beef steak, thinly sliced
    1/2 pint oysters, shucked
    10 or more fresh small clams, well scrubbed
    1 pound squid, cleaned and cut in
        1-inch pieces
    1/2 pound raw shrimp, shelled and
        deveined
    1/2 pound chicken livers, halved
    1/2 pound pork kidneys, white core
        discarded, thinly sliced
    1 pound Napa cabbage, cut in bite-size
        pieces
    1 pound spinach, ends trimmed
    4 fresh bean-curd cakes, cut in 1-inch pieces
    8 ounces bean-thread noodles, soaked to
        soften and cut in 6-inch lengths
condiments for dipping sauce:
    light soy sauce, fish soy, oyster sauce,
        hoisin sauce
    chili oil, Oriental sesame oil, hot mustard,
        sesame-seed paste
    rice wine or dry sherry, brewed tea for
        diluting (at room temperature)
    minced garlic, chopped Chinese chives,
        minced ginger root, chopped green
        onions, chopped coriander
    beaten eggs
    salt, sugar

MONGOLIAN FIREPOT

for broth:
    3 quarts water
    2 slices ginger root
    2 green onions
platters of:
    4 pounds boneless lamb or tender beef,
        thinly sliced
    1 pound Napa cabbage, cut in bite-size
        pieces
    1 pound spinach, ends trimmed
    8 ounces bean-thread noodles, soaked to
        soften and cut in 6-inch lengths
condiments for dipping sauce:
    light soy sauce, fish soy, oyster sauce,
        hoisin sauce
    chili oil, Oriental sesame oil, hot mustard,
        sesame-seed paste
    rice wine or dry sherry, brewed tea for
        diluting (at room temperature)
    minced garlic, chopped Chinese chives,
        minced ginger root, chopped green
        onions, chopped coriander
    beaten eggs
    salt, sugar

DIM SUM

Some of the most delightful "dining out"—Chinese style—has not been done in restaurants, but in teahouses, which in Old China were open from early morning till late at night. Just as tea was not generally served at main meals, those exquisite appetizers, dim sum, did not introduce a dinner. Literally meaning "touch the heart," they were meant to be enjoyed at odd moments whenever the heart desired. These delicate dumplings were designed to be served in small, yet satisfying amounts to the accompaniment of refreshing tea, and could be filled with meat, seafood or vegetables, sweet paste or preserves.

Today special dim sum restaurants, usually open in the middle of the day from 10 am till 2 pm, can be found in many cities outside of China. Carts filled with a fascinating variety are wheeled from table to table, and it's easy to get carried away trying every kind. Customers usually end up with a rather substantial brunch or lunch. At home, cooks find that, in spite of tradition, dim sum make excellent hors d'oeuvre.

Tea can be made from flowers, leaves, roots, seeds or berries of many plants, but of course is primarily associated with leaves of the tea plant, a shrub of the camellia family that thrives in some of the higher elevations of southern Asia. Starting as a medicine sometime before 350 B.C., it became firmly established as a popular beverage in China by the eighth century, not only because of its flavor, but also because of the stimulating effect of its caffeine content.

Leaves are graded by size. The smallest yield gunpowder tea, which tends to be somewhat bitter; the largest, hyson tea, which is much lighter. Immediately after picking, the leaves are steamed to sterilize, rolled lightly to break up the cells, then heated to dry and preserve color. This process produces green tea. For two other types the leaves are first withered and made pliable by long, low heating and then rolled and twisted into lumps. A roller-breaker breaks the leaves for sifting, after which the tea is spread on frames, covered with wet cloths and allowed to ferment. Short fermentation gives red, or oolong tea; long produces black tea. Fermentation is stopped by heating and drying.

159

DIM SUM

Flavors vary widely depending on where the tea was grown and how it was processed and blended. During the Sung Dynasty (960 to 1368), leaves were formed into tablets to be chewed while sipping hot water, or pressed into bricks for transporting and storage. Tea was so precious that the bricks were used as money. The fragrance and flavor of some teas are further enhanced by the addition of blossoms or fruit. *Mook lay faah cha*, jasmine tea, is a black tea with the delicate flavoring of jasmine flowers; *luy jee cha*, lichee tea, a black tea to which lichees are added. *Po nay cha*, a reddish-black tea from the province of Yunnan, is combined with small, white chrysanthemum buds to make the very popular chrysanthemum tea, a beverage particularly enjoyed with rich foods and dim sum. Chrysanthemum tea is also one Chinese tea to which sugar is often added. Scents of gardenia, lavender, magnolia, orange blossoms and mint may also be added.

Several provinces of China are recognized for their production of especially fine teas. *Taw cha*, a strong brick tea, comes from the province of Szechwan. Fukien contributes two excellent red teas: *mo yee cha* and *teet gwoon yun cha* (iron goddess of mercy tea). Two green teas from Chinkiang, renowned for their delicate flavor and pleasing fragrance, are *heung pien cha* (fragrant petals tea) and *loong jan cha* (dragon's well tea). Green teas grown in the province of Kwangtung include *suy sien cha* (water nymph tea), *loong so cha* (dragon's beard tea), *ngun jum cha* (silver needles tea) and *sao may cha* (eyebrows of longevity tea). Also from Kwangtung comes *oolong cha* (black dragon tea), the blackish-red tea that is most widely served in Chinese homes.

Brewing good tea requires a teapot of porcelain or earthenware, not metal, and fresh, pure water brought to a bubble, not a boil. Rinse out the pot with scalding water before pouring the bubbling water over the tea leaves, about a cup to a teaspoon of leaves. Steeping takes around three minutes.

Tea should be kept in an airtight container. Some claim tea does not improve with age like wine. This may be true of unfermented varieties, but one who has the rare opportunity of tasting a most delicious, mellow, black tea made with shavings from a brick 50 years old will completely disagree when it comes to fermented types.

BASIC STEAMED BREAD

Steamed breads are a staple food of Northern China where wheat flour is abundant. The dough is made into buns; they may be in fancy shapes, plain or stuffed.

4 cups unbleached flour
1 teaspoon salt
1/4 cup sugar
1 tablespoon active dry yeast
1-1/2 cups warm water
2 tablespoons peanut oil or melted lard

In bowl combine flour and salt. Dissolve sugar and yeast in water until bubbly. Add oil to yeast mixture and slowly add to flour, blending well with chopsticks or fork. Turn out onto lightly floured board and knead 15 minutes or until smooth and elastic. Place in greased bowl, cover with dampened tea towel and let rise in warm place 1 to 1-1/2 hours or until double in bulk. Turn out onto floured board and knead 2 or 3 minutes. Shape into round buns, place each on a square of wax paper and place in bamboo steamer or flat dish or pan. Cover and let rise again 45 minutes or until double in bulk. Steam above boiling water 20 minutes. Serve hot.
Yield: 20 to 24 buns

JAO TZE DOUGH
Peking

2 cups unbleached flour
1/2 teaspoon salt
approximately 3/4 cup hot water

Combine flour and salt. Gradually add hot water, stirring constantly with chopsticks or fork to form dough. Turn out on floured board and knead 5 minutes. Cover with dampened tea towel and let rest 20 minutes. Knead again for 5 minutes and roll into ropes 1 inch in diameter. Cut into 40 1-inch pieces. Roll out each piece into a 3-inch circle, keeping remaining pieces covered with tea towel. Fill with desired filling and fold in desired shape.
Yield: approximately 40 rounds
Note Gyoza skins or the thicker round won ton skins may be used for jao tze rounds. They may be purchased in Oriental markets and some supermarkets and are slightly thicker than square won ton skins. A 1-pound package yields approximately 40 skins.
To Make Bonnet Shape Make 4 pleats on one half of skin. Bring other half of skin up to form a pocket and fill with 1 tablespoon filling. Bring flap up and over to enclose filling and pinch edges together.

FUN GOH DOUGH

2-1/2 cups (1 pound) wheat starch* or
   fine cake flour
1 teaspoon salt
approximately 2 cups boiling water
peanut oil

In large bowl combine wheat starch and salt. Gradually add boiling water, stirring constantly with chopsticks or fork. Form into ball and knead in the bowl for 5 minutes. Form into ball and rub lightly with oil. Cover with dampened tea towel and let rest 30 minutes. Lightly oil a pastry board to prevent sticking and with hands roll dough into ropes 1 inch in diameter. Cut off 1-inch pieces and roll each piece with a rolling pin into a 3-inch circle. Or use the flat side of a lightly oiled cleaver and press down to flatten dough. Fill with desired filling and form into desired shape.
Yield: 4 to 5 dozen rounds
*Available in Oriental markets

SPRING ROLL SKINS
Shanghai

1 cup unbleached flour
1/2 teaspoon salt
2 eggs, beaten
approximately 2 cups water
vegetable oil

Sift flour and salt into mixing bowl. Add eggs and enough water to make a smooth, thin batter similar to crêpe batter. Always beat batter in one direction to gain elasticity. Let stand 20 minutes. Lightly oil a 6-inch skillet or crêpe pan and heat over low heat. Beat batter in same direction and pour 2 tablespoons into pan, tilting pan to cover entire surface with batter. Cook until set. Pancake should be sheer and pliable. When it shrinks away slightly from the edges, turn over and cook other side just to set. Remove to flat dish, cover with slightly dampened tea towel and repeat with remaining batter, oiling pan as necessary and being sure to stir in one direction each time.
Yield: approximately 18 spring roll skins
Note Spring roll skins are also known as Shanghai-type spring roll skins and are available in some Oriental markets. Lumpia skins, available in Philippine markets, may be substituted. Egg roll skins may also be substituted, but they are much thicker.

WON TON DOUGH

3 cups unbleached flour
1 teaspoon salt
1 egg, lightly beaten
about 1/2 cup water
cornstarch for dusting

Combine flour and salt and mound on pastry board. Make an indentation in center of mound, add egg and mix with fingers. Gradually add water to form dough. Knead 10 minutes and form into a ball. Cover with a dampened tea towel and let rest 20 minutes. Roll out in several batches to desired thickness, in most cases as thinly as possible. Cut in 4-inch squares or 3-inch rounds. Dust dough pieces lightly with cornstarch, stack and cover with cloth to prevent drying out until ready to fill.
Yield: 1 pound, approximately 40 skins

DIPPING SAUCE

For dumplings, shui mai, jao tze, kuoteh, boiled noodles.

1/3 cup dark or light soy sauce
1/3 cup rice vinegar
2 to 3 slices ginger root, minced (optional)
2 to 3 garlic cloves, minced
2 teaspoons Oriental sesame oil
1 teaspoon chili oil (optional)
1/2 teaspoon sugar

Combine all ingredients and let stand 10 minutes to blend flavors.

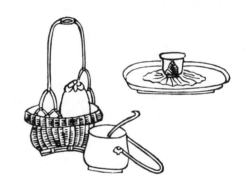

CHA SIEW BAO
(Steamed Buns with Pork Filling)

1 recipe basic steamed bread (page 161)
1/2 pound Chinese barbecued pork, diced
1/4 cup chopped green onion
1 tablespoon brown bean sauce
1 tablespoon oyster sauce
1 tablespoon hoisin sauce
1 tablespoon sugar
1/2 teaspoon five-spice powder
2 tablespoons peanut oil
1/2 cup diced bamboo shoots
1/3 cup water
binder of:
   2 tablespoons water
   1 tablespoon cornstarch
1 teaspoon Oriental sesame oil
1 tablespoon chopped coriander leaves

Combine barbecued pork, onion, brown bean sauce, oyster sauce, hoisin sauce, sugar and five-spice powder. Heat peanut oil in wok or skillet and stir-fry meat mixture and bamboo shoots 30 seconds. Add water. Bring just to boil, bind with cornstarch mixture and remove from heat. Blend in sesame oil and chopped coriander. Fill and steam as for gai bao, following.

GAI BAO
(Steamed Buns with Chicken Filling)
Canton

1 recipe basic steamed bread (page 161)
2 cups diced raw chicken meat
4 to 6 dried forest mushrooms, soaked to soften and diced
1 teaspoon minced ginger root
1 tablespoon cornstarch
1 tablespoon oyster sauce or hoisin sauce
2 tablespoons chopped green onion or Chinese chives
1/4 teaspoon five-spice powder
3 tablespoons peanut oil
1/2 cup hot chicken stock
1/2 teaspoon Oriental sesame oil

Combine chicken, mushrooms, ginger, cornstarch, oyster sauce, green onions and five-spice powder. Heat oil in wok or skillet and stir-fry chicken mixture 1 minute or until chicken begins to lose its pinkness. Add stock and cook another minute. Remove from heat and add sesame oil. Cool. Divide bread dough into 16 pieces after first rising. Roll each into a 4-inch circle 1/4 inch thick. Place 1 tablespoon of chicken filling in center and bring outer edges together to enclose filling. Twist top to seal. Place on a 4-inch square of wax paper and repeat with remaining dough. Follow directions for rising and steaming for basic steamed bread.
Yield: 16 to 20 buns

D
I
M
S
U
M

POT STICKERS WITH
BEEF AND WATER CHESTNUTS
Shanghai

1 recipe jao tze dough (page 161)
filling:
  1 pound lean ground beef
  3/4 cup minced water chestnuts
  1 piece dried tangerine peel, soaked to
    soften and minced
  2 tablespoons minced coriander leaves
  1 teaspoon minced ginger root
  1 tablespoon cornstarch
  1 tablespoon soy sauce
  1/2 teaspoon each sugar and salt
  1/2 teaspoon Oriental sesame oil

Combine filling ingredients and let stand 20 minutes to blend flavors. Roll dough as directed and fill, making bonnet shape (page 161). Place on oiled pan in one layer and steam over boiling water 15 minutes.

JAO TZE
Peking

1 recipe jao tze dough (page 161)
filling:
  1 pound lean ground pork butt or beef
  2 slices ginger root, minced
  2 green onions, minced
  1 cup blanched, chopped Napa cabbage
    or spinach
  1 tablespoon soy sauce
  2 teaspoons rice wine or dry sherry
  1 tablespoon cornstarch
  1/2 teaspoon Oriental sesame oil
for dipping:
  rice vinegar
  chili oil
  soy sauce

Combine filling ingredients and let stand 20 minutes to blend flavors. Roll and cut dough skins as directed. Fill and shape into bonnet shape (page 161). Bring 3 quarts water to boil, add jao tze and bring water back to boil. Immediately add 1 cup cold water. Bring back to boil and remove with strainer. Serve with rice vinegar, chili oil and soy sauce.

KUOTEH OR POT STICKERS
(FRIED JAO TZE)

Prepare jao tze, preceding, but do not cook. Heat 2 flat-bottomed skillets until very hot and add 2 tablespoons peanut oil to each skillet. Place jao tze in skillets in one layer. Cover and heat over low heat 5 minutes or until browned. Add 1/3 cup stock or water to each skillet, cover and cook 5 minutes or longer until liquid has completely evaporated. Turn out onto warm platter browned side up and serve.

D I M S U M

STUFFED BAMBOO LEAVES WITH GLUTINOUS RICE, CHINESE SAUSAGE AND CHESTNUTS

2 dozen dried bamboo leaves*
6 cups cooked glutinous rice (page 65)
4 Chinese sausage, cut in thirds
12 dried chestnuts, parboiled 15 minutes
    and drained
6 dried forest mushrooms, soaked to soften
    and halved

Soak bamboo leaves at least 4 hours. Wash and drain. Lay 12 of the leaves flat on board. Place 1/2 cup cooked rice in center and pat down to flatten. Place a piece of sausage, a chestnut and a mushroom half on top. Fold over in thirds to enclose filling without folding in sides. Filling will show but remain intact. Line a bamboo steamer basket with some of the remaining bamboo leaves to completely cover bottom and sides, reserving enough leaves to cover top. Place filled leaves seam side down in lined steamer. Top with remaining bamboo leaves, making sure all rolls are well covered. The leaves will impart a delicate flavor to the filling. Steam above boiling water 1 hour. Serve hot and let guests open their own package.
Yield: 12
*Available in Chinese markets. Parchment paper or corn leaves may be substituted, but will not impart the flavor which makes these so unique and delicious.

HAR GOW
(Shrimp and Bamboo
Shoot Filling)
Canton

1 recipe fun goh dough (page 162)
filling:
    1 pound raw shrimp, shelled, deveined and
        minced
    1 cup minced bamboo shoots
    2 tablespoons cornstarch
    1 tablespoon light soy sauce
    1 tablespoon rice wine or dry sherry
    1/2 teaspoon salt
    1/2 teaspoon Oriental sesame oil
peanut oil

Combine filling ingredients and let stand 20 minutes to blend flavors. Roll out and cut fun goh dough as directed in recipe. Fill and form into bonnet shape (page 161). Place har gow on oiled shallow heatproof pan or oiled steamer rack. Repeat with remaining skins and filling. Steam above boiling water for 15 minutes. Remove from heat, brush with a little peanut oil to keep skin from drying out and give a shiny appearance. Serve hot.
Yield: 48 har gow
Variation Omit bamboo shoots. Add 3/4 cup minced water chestnuts, 1 teaspoon minced ginger root and 2 tablespoons minced green onion.

PORK, DRIED SHRIMP AND MUSHROOM FUN GOH

1 recipe fun goh dough (page 162)
filling:
    2 tablespoons peanut oil
    1/4 cup dried shrimp, soaked to soften
      and minced
    4 dried forest mushrooms, soaked to
      soften and minced
    1/2 pound lean ground pork butt
    1 piece dried tangerine peel, soaked to
      soften and minced
    6 to 8 water chestnuts, minced
    1 tablespoon soy sauce
    2 teaspoons rice wine or dry sherry
    1/4 teaspoon five-spice powder
    binder of:
      2 tablespoons water
      1 tablespoon cornstarch
    1/4 cup minced green onion
    1/2 teaspoon Oriental sesame oil
    salt to taste
peanut oil

Heat 2 tablespoons peanut oil in wok or skillet. Stir-fry shrimp and mushrooms 30 seconds. Add pork and stir-fry another 30 seconds. Add tangerine peel, water chestnuts, soy, wine and five-spice powder. Cover and let steam rise to surface. Bind with cornstarch mixture and add onions, sesame oil and salt. Cool before filling. Roll out and cut fun goh dough as directed in recipe. Fill and form into bonnet shape (page 161). Place fun goh on oiled shallow heatproof pan or oiled steamer. Repeat with remaining skins and filling. Steam above boiling water for 15 minutes. Remove from heat, brush with a little peanut oil to keep skin from drying out and give a shiny appearance. Serve hot.
Yield: 48 fun goh

D I M S U M

PORK AND SHRIMP WON TON FILLING

1 pound won ton skins
filling:
- 1/2 pound lean ground pork butt
- 1/2 pound raw shrimp, shelled, deveined and minced
- 2 tablespoons cornstarch
- 1 or 2 green onions, minced
- 1 tablespoon soy sauce
- 1/2 teaspoon Oriental sesame oil
- 1/2 teaspoon salt
- 1 egg, beaten

Combine filling ingredients and let stand 15 minutes to blend flavors. Fill and fold won ton skins as directed on page 172 and parboil for soup, or deep-fry or steam for appetizer.
Variations Any one or combination of the following ingredients may be added to the filling.
- 1/2 cup minced water chestnuts
- 4 to 6 dried forest mushrooms, soaked to soften and minced
- 1 piece dried tangerine peel, soaked to soften and minced
- 2 tablespoons minced fresh coriander
- 1/2 cup blanched shredded Napa cabbage or spinach

PORK AND SHRIMP SHUI MAI

1/2 pound round won ton skins
filling:
    1/2 pound lean ground pork butt
    1/2 pound raw shrimp, shelled, deveined
      and minced
    1 tablespoon rice wine or dry sherry
    2 tablespoons cornstarch
    2 tablespoons water
    1/2 teaspoon each sugar and salt
    1 tablespoon light soy sauce
    1/2 teaspoon Oriental sesame oil
    2 tablespoons minced green onion
garnish of:
    coriander leaves, or
    fresh green peas, or
    slivers of softened dried forest mushrooms,
      or
    slivered water chestnuts

Combine filling ingredients and let stand 15 minutes to blend flavors. Place a full tablespoon of filling on each won ton round. Bring all edges upward toward center, forming little pleats and leaving meat exposed on top. Flatten bottom so shui mai will stand up. Place a small bit of garnish on meat and transfer to oiled pan. Steam above boiling water 20 minutes. Serve immediately or make ahead and reheat in steamer.
Yield: 20 shui mai

BEEF SHUI MAI

1/2 pound round won ton skins
filling:
    1 pound lean ground beef
    1 tablespoon minced ginger root
    1/4 cup minced green onion
    2 tablespoons soy sauce, or
    1 tablespoon each soy sauce and
      oyster sauce
    1 piece dried tangerine peel, soaked to
      soften and minced
    2 tablespoons cornstarch
    2 tablespoons water
    1/2 teaspoon sugar
    1/2 teaspoon black pepper

Combine filling ingredients and let stand 15 minutes to blend flavors. Place a tablespoon of filling on each won ton skin and completely enclose filling, forming a small ball and pinching to seal. Place smooth surface up on oiled plate. Repeat with remaining filling and skins and steam above boiling water 15 minutes. Serve immediately or make ahead and reheat in steamer.
Yield: 20 shui mai

D
I
M
S
U
M

D I M S U M

FRIED WON TON

1 pound square won ton skins
peanut oil for deep-frying

Curried Beef Filling

  3/4 pound lean ground beef
  1/4 cup finely minced bell pepper
  1/4 cup finely minced green onion
  2 slices ginger root, minced
  1 tablespoon curry powder
  1 tablespoon salt
  1/2 teaspoon Oriental sesame oil
  2 tablespoons cornstarch
  1 egg, beaten

Shrimp Filling

  3/4 pound raw shrimp, shelled, deveined
    and minced
  1/2 cup finely minced water chestnuts
  2 tablespoons minced green onion
  1/2 teaspoon Oriental sesame oil
  2 teaspoons light soy sauce
  1/2 teaspoon rice wine or dry sherry
  1/4 teaspoon five-spice powder
  1/4 teaspoon white pepper
  2 tablespoons cornstarch
  1 egg, beaten

Combine ingredients for beef filling and for shrimp filling and let each stand 10 minutes to blend flavors. Place a teaspoonful of filling in center of won ton skin. Fold in half to form a triangle and bring opposite points together. Pinch to hold or seal with a dab of water. Repeat with remaining filling and skins. Deep-fry a few at a time in hot oil until lightly golden. Drain and serve immediately. *Note* Both fillings may be used for soup won tons. If using beef filling, omit curry powder.

Variations for Shrimp Filling

Omit soy sauce and add 2 teaspoons hoisin
  sauce
Substitute raw ground fish for the shrimp
Substitute 1/2 pound ground pork butt for
  1/2 pound of the shrimp
Substitute minced raw chicken breast meat
  for the shrimp

SPRING ROLLS
Shanghai

1 tablespoon peanut oil
2 celery ribs, sliced thinly on diagonal
1 pound mung bean sprouts
3/4 cup matchstick-cut bamboo shoots
1/4 cup matchstick-cut water chestnuts
2 teaspoons light soy sauce
1/2 teaspoon sugar
1/2 pound flaked crab meat
1/2 teaspoon Oriental sesame oil
2 tablespoons minced green onion
2 tablespoons cornstarch
egg slivers made with 2 eggs (page 50)
1 recipe spring roll skins (page 162), or
1 1-pound package spring-roll skins
coriander sprigs
peanut oil for deep-frying
Chinese mustard
chili oil
soy sauce

Heat peanut oil in wok or skillet and stir-fry celery, bean sprouts, bamboo shoots, water chestnuts, soy and sugar 2 minutes. Stir in crab and remove from heat. Pour off any juices and add sesame oil, green onion, cornstarch and egg slivers. Cool and place 3 tablespoons of mixture on edge of spring roll skin. Place a coriander sprig on top and fold skin over twice. Then fold in sides and roll like jelly roll. Deep-fry, seam side down, in hot oil until crisp and golden. Drain, cut into 1-inch slices and serve immediately with mustard, chili oil and soy.
Yield: approximately 18 spring rolls

SHRIMP TOAST
Shanghai

1/2 pound raw shrimp, shelled, deveined and minced
2 tablespoons finely minced Virginia ham (optional)
6 to 8 water chestnuts, minced
1 tablespoon minced green onion
1 teaspoon minced ginger root
2 teaspoons cornstarch
1 teaspoon rice wine or dry sherry
1/2 teaspoon salt
1/2 teaspoon white pepper
1 egg, beaten
dash of Oriental sesame oil
4 slices stale white bread, crusts removed
peanut oil for deep-frying

Combine shrimp, ham, water chestnuts, green onion, ginger root, cornstarch, wine, salt, pepper, egg and sesame oil. Spread evenly on one side of each slice of bread. Cut into 4 triangles and drop triangles, shrimp mixture side down, into hot oil. Fry until golden, turn and brown other side. Drain on paper toweling and serve immediately, or make ahead and reheat in 275° oven 15 minutes.

SWEETS

STEAMED SPONGE CAKE
Canton

6 eggs, separated
1 cup sugar
1 teaspoon almond extract
2 tablespoons water
1-1/2 cups flour
1/2 teaspoon baking powder
1/2 teaspoon salt

Beat egg whites until fluffy. Continue beating, gradually adding sugar, and beat until stiff. Set aside. Beat yolks with almond extract until light and yellow. Add water and fold into whites just to blend. Sift together flour, baking powder and salt. Gradually fold into egg mixture. Line an 8-inch square pan with waxed paper. Pour in cake batter and steam over gently boiling water 30 minutes, or until toothpick inserted in center comes out clean. Serve hot or cold.

Variation Add 1/2 cup shredded coconut to the batter.

ALMOND COOKIES

1 cup lard
1 cup sugar, or
1/2 cup each white sugar and brown sugar
1 egg, beaten
1/2 cup ground blanched almonds
1 teaspoon almond extract
2-1/2 cups flour
1-1/2 teaspoons baking powder
1/2 teaspoon salt
3 dozen blanched almond halves
glaze mixture of:
   1 egg yolk
   1 tablespoon water

Cream together lard and sugar until smooth. Blend in egg, almonds and almond extract. Sift together flour, baking powder and salt. Gradually blend into egg mixture; dough will be stiff. Shape into 1-inch balls. Place 2 inches apart on greased cookie sheet. Press an almond half on each cookie and flatten each cookie to 1/2-inch thickness. Brush with egg yolk glaze and bake in preheated 350° oven 20 minutes or until lightly golden.
Yield: 3 dozen

SESAME SEED COOKIES

1/2 cup lard or shortening
3/4 cup sugar
2 eggs
1 teaspoon Oriental sesame oil
2 cups flour
1 teaspoon baking powder
1/2 teaspoon salt
1 cup toasted sesame seeds

Cream together lard and sugar until smooth. Beat in eggs and sesame oil. Sift flour, baking powder and salt together and blend into lard-sugar mixture. Shape into 1-inch balls and roll balls in sesame seeds, pressing in firmly. Place on greased baking sheet and flatten each ball to 1/2-inch thickness. Bake in preheated 350° oven 20 minutes.
Yield: 2-1/2 dozen

WATER CHESTNUT PUDDING

A cool and refreshing dessert or snack.

3 cups water
1/2 cup sugar
1 stick agar-agar, cut up
1 teaspoon almond extract
1 cup finely minced water chestnuts
peanut oil

Combine water, sugar and agar-agar and let stand 5 minutes to dissolve. Over medium heat, bring just to boil and simmer 10 minutes. Add almond extract and water chestnuts. Oil a shallow dish with peanut oil and pour in agar-agar mixture. Cool and refrigerate to set. Cut into 2-inch diamonds.

DRAGON EYE PUDDING
Shanghai

1 13-ounce can longans (dragon's eyes)
2 tablespoons rice flour

Drain longans and reserve enough syrup, adding water if needed, to make 2 cups. Combine with rice flour in saucepan. Bring to gentle boil, stirring constantly, and cook until thickened. Add longans and serve in individual bowls, hot or at room temperature.
Variation Lichees may be substituted for the longans.

ALMOND FLOAT
Canton

2 tablespoons unflavored gelatin
1 cup cold water
1/3 cup sugar
3 cups milk at room temperature
1-1/2 teaspoons almond extract
fresh or canned fruits

Sprinkle gelatin over water to soften. Add sugar and heat over medium heat, stirring constantly, to dissolve gelatin. Bring just to boil, remove from heat and gradually add milk, stirring constantly. Add almond extract and pour into a 6-cup mold or individual dishes. Cool and chill until firm. Serve with fresh fruits and their juices (pineapple, berries, peaches, melon balls) or canned fruits and juices (longans, lichees, mandarin oranges).

ALMOND TEA

1/2 cup rice, washed and well drained
1-1/2 cups blanched almonds
4 cups water
1/4 cup sugar
1/2 teaspoon almond extract

Put rice and almonds into a blender. Adding just enough of the water to purée mixture, blend until smooth. Rice must be thoroughly pulverized. Pour mixture from blender and remaining water into a saucepan. Over medium heat, cook, stirring constantly, 25 minutes or until thickened. Then add sugar and almond extract, stirring in well. Pour into 6 individual cups and sip or eat with a porcelain spoon as a light dessert.

SWEET EGG FLOWER TEA
Hunan

3 cups water
1/2 cup rock sugar
3 eggs, lightly beaten
2 tablespoons rice wine

Bring water to boil, add rock sugar and bring back to boil. Lower heat and simmer, stirring, until sugar is dissolved. Gradually add beaten eggs in a thin stream, stirring very gently with chopsticks until all egg has been added. Stir in rice wine. Serve immediately in soup bowls with porcelain spoons. A refreshing and soothing sweet.

FRIED FRUIT PUFFS
Peking

1/2 cup each pitted dates, dried apricots,
    candied orange peel and raisins
1/2 cup shredded coconut
1 tablespoon toasted sesame seeds
1/3 cup peanut butter (preferably chunky
    style)
2 egg whites, beaten slightly
1/2 cup cornstarch
peanut oil for deep-frying
sugar for coating

Mince or grind dates, apricots, orange peel and raisins. Combine with coconut, sesame seeds and peanut butter. Form into 1-inch balls and dip in egg white. Roll in cornstarch and deep-fry a few at a time until golden. Drain on paper toweling and roll in sugar. Or keep hot in oven and roll in sugar just before serving. May be eaten at room temperature. Yield: 3 dozen

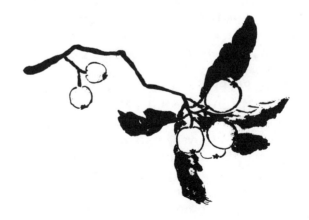

GLOSSARY

AGAR-AGAR Also called kanten. A gelatin substance made from the gum of seaweed. It comes in 3 forms: powdered, 1-inch thick by 10-inch long sticks, and thin, transparent noodle-like strips. Soak in *cold* water just to soften. For salads, soak in cold water 10 minutes, rinse well and drain. Sold by weight.

ANCIENT EGGS, PRESERVED Also called thousand-year eggs. Duck eggs with a black, mud coating of ashes, lime and salt, aged by burying for 100 days. Inside of egg becomes firm and a grayish-green color from aging. Smoky, delicate flavor. Sold individually in Oriental markets. (See recipe, page 47.)

ANISE PEPPER See Szechwan Peppercorns.

BALSAM PEAR See Bitter Melon.

BAMBOO SHOOTS Available water-packed in cans in two varieties: spring, which are large and fine for cutting into matchstick or for slicing; winter, which are smaller, smoother in texture, very tender and more expensive. After opening, drain, cover with cold water and store in the refrigerator.

BAMBOO SHOOTS, SALTED Available in cans, thinly sliced and packed in salt brine. They have a distinct flavor and are most often used for steamed meat dishes. Rinse in cold water before using.

BANANA FLOWERS See Golden Needles.

BEAN CAKE, FERMENTED Beige-colored, pressed bean-curd cake in a fermented rice wine with salt. Quite pungent; similar to a Brie cheese. Used as a sauce when cooked, or may be eaten straight from the jar with hot rice or rice crusts. Available in jars; reserve liquid and use in recipes. Taste mellows with aging and color becomes darker. Store in cool cupboard. Available with chili pepper added.

BEAN-CURD CAKE, FRESH Made from puréed soybeans, then formed into 2-inch squares, 1 inch thick. Comes in firm and soft forms. Firmer cakes are preferred for stir-fry dishes because they hold their shape during cooking. Softer cakes are preferred for soups and cold dishes because of their smoother texture. Place in fresh cold water after purchasing, changing water daily and storing in the refrigerator. Use within 2 to 3 days of purchase. Rinse under cold water before using. Readily available in supermarkets.

BEAN-CURD CHEESE, RED (NAM GOOEY) Pressed bean-curd cakes in fermented rice wine, spices and salt. Liquid is brownish-red; strong and pungent. Available in cans. To store, put in glass jar with lid and refrigerate.

BEAN-CURD CAKE, DEEP-FRIED Bean-curd cakes that have been cubed and deep-fried. (See recipe, page 58.)

BEAN-CURD SHEETS OR STICKS, DRIED Creamy beige-colored thin sheets. Used for vegetarian (Buddhist) dishes, congee or as substitute for egg roll skins. Stick form is used mainly for soup. Both types have a slightly chewy texture after cooking. Always soak in warm water to make pliable before proceeding with recipe. Available in Oriental markets.

BEAN CURD, SWEET Comes in dried, flat sheets, about 6 inches by 1-1/2 inches. Mocha in color; no sweet taste.

BEAN PASTE, HOT See Hot Bean Paste.

BEAN-THREAD NOODLES Often called cellophane or pea starch noodles. Dry, thin, translucent noodles made from ground mung beans. Must always be soaked in warm water to soften (about 10 minutes) before using. Sold by weight (2 to 8 ounces) in looped skeins in Oriental markets.

BITTER MELON (BALSAM PEAR) Light green, cucumber-like, wrinkled vegetable with a shiny skin. Quite perishable. The bitter taste is because of the quinine in the vegetable. Blanch quickly to release some of the bitterness. Discard pulp and seeds.

BLACK BEANS, FERMENTED Small black beans preserved in salt. Very pungent and moist. Almost always used with garlic and ginger in sauces. Rinse with warm water and mash before using. Purchased in plastic bags by weight in Oriental markets.

BOK CHOY See Chinese Chard.

BROWN BEAN SAUCE Also known as yellow bean sauce and ground bean sauce. Brown or yellowish thick, salty bean sauce made of ground or partially mashed beans. Made from yellow beans, flour and salt and then fermented. Available in cans and jars. Should be stored in a jar in the refrigerator or a cool cupboard. Available in Oriental markets.

CELERY CABBAGE See Napa Cabbage.

CELLOPHANE NOODLES See Bean-Thread Noodles.

CHA SIEW See Chinese Barbecued Pork.

CHESTNUTS, DRIED Nuts that have been shelled, fried and halved. Same as American variety. Sold by weight in Oriental markets.

CHILI OIL Called aji oil in Japanese markets. Reddish oil flavored with hot peppers. Available in bottles in Oriental markets. To make your own: Heat 1 cup peanut oil until it just begins to smoke. Remove from heat and add 1/4 cup cayenne pepper or powdered red pepper, blending well. Cool and store in a glass jar with a tight-fitting lid. For extra flavor, substitute 1/4 cup or more Oriental sesame oil for an equal amount of the peanut oil.

CHILI PEPPERS, DRIED RED Very hot, small chilis. Use sparingly. Discard seeds if less hotness is desired. Fresh green chili peppers, any variety, may be substituted.

CHILI PEPPERS, HOT GREEN Any variety of fresh hot green chili pepper may be used. Use cautiously; hotness of varieties varies.

CHINESE BARBECUED PORK (CHA SIEW) Sweet, reddish-brown roast pork sold by weight. (See recipe, page 142.)

CHINESE BROCCOLI (GAI LAHN) Similar to American broccoli, but longer, thinner stalks, more leafy greens and less flowers.

Glossary

CHINESE CABBAGE See Napa Cabbage.

CHINESE CHARD (BOK CHOY) Leafy dark green vegetable with white stem. Most popular Chinese green vegetable. The heart or center stem and the leaves and their flowers are often sold separately in Chinese markets. The young tender shoots or the heart are the best.

CHINESE CHIVES Similar to American chives, with narrow, flat, thin blades. Distinct sharp, pungent flavor. Sold fresh all year. Member of the onion family; easily grown from seed.

CHINESE LETTUCE See Napa Cabbage.

CHINESE MUSTARD, DRY Used at the table as a condiment. Available in tins by the ounce at Oriental markets. To make: Combine equal amounts of dry mustard and water to make a smooth consistency. Add a drop of Oriental sesame oil. Let stand 30 minutes to mellow flavors. If Chinese mustard is unavailable, Colman's English dry mustard may be substituted.

CHINESE MUSTARD GREENS (GAI CHOY) Leafy yellow-green vegetable similar to but less bitter than American variety. Thick-stalked variety has more crunch and is the only one recommended for pickling.

CHINESE OKRA Also called silk squash or silk melon. Vegetable similar to cucumber but shaped more like a long okra with ridges. Delicate, sweet taste. Available from spring to early fall.

CHINESE PARSLEY See Coriander, Fresh.

CHINESE PRESERVED TURNIPS (CHOONG TOY) Rolled up bundles of salted, moist turnips with tops. Used as a flavoring. To use, unroll bundles, rinse well and chop. Comes by weight in plastic packages. Transfer to airtight container to prevent drying out. Store in cool place or refrigerate. May also be purchased flat.

CHINESE SAUSAGE (LOP CHIANG) Cured sweet pork sausage. Must be cooked before eating. About 6 inches in length and sold by weight loose in some markets, or in 1-pound packages. Refrigerate or freeze.

CHINESE TURNIPS Large, long white turnips similar to a white radish. Stronger taste than American variety. Substitute Japanese daikon. Available in Chinese markets all year, but best in winter.

CHOONG TOY See Chinese Preserved Turnips.

CLOUD EARS Small, dried grayish-brown fungus. Shaped like a small ear after soaked in warm water to soften. Expands to 5 times its size when soaked. Remove any tough stems. Delicate taste with a light crisp texture. Sold by weight in packages at Oriental markets.

CORIANDER, FRESH Also called Chinese parsley and cilantro. Green, flat-leaved herb similar in appearance to Italian parsley. Strong, aromatic flavor. Use sparingly when adding to recipes. Often an acquired taste though used widely by the Chinese to garnish almost any dish.

DRAGON'S EYES (LONGANS) Transparent, whitish fruit subtly fragrant and sweet, about the size of a grape. Related to the lichee family. Available ready to eat in cans packed in light syrup.

DRIED CHESTNUTS See Chestnuts, Dried.

DRIED FOREST MUSHROOMS See Forest Mushrooms, Dried.

DRIED OYSTERS See Oysters, Dried.

DRIED SEAWEED See Seaweed, Dried.

DRIED SHRIMP See Shrimp, Dried.

DRIED TANGERINE PEEL See Tangerine Peel, Dried.

FERMENTED BEAN CAKE See Bean Cake, Fermented.

FERMENTED BLACK BEANS See Black Beans, Fermented.

FISH SOY Light sauce made with fish extract, water and salt. Smells like canned anchovies. Use sparingly. Sold in bottles.

FIVE-SPICE POWDER A combination of star anise, Szechwan peppercorns, fennel, cloves and cinnamon. Fragrant and pungent. Sold packaged or in small jars.

FOREST MUSHROOMS, DRIED Brownish-black Oriental mushrooms available in thin (1/8 inch thick) and thick (1/2 inch thick) varieties. The thick ones have a cracked look to the surface of the cap, are more expensive and meatier. The thin variety is better for stir-fried dishes, good for flavoring soups and considerably less expensive. Soak in warm water to soften before using. Sold by weight in Oriental markets.

FUZZY MELON An oblong, green vegetable of the squash family with fuzz on the outside. Always scrape or peel before using. Available in spring to early fall.

GAI CHOY See Chinese Mustard Greens.

GAI LAHN See Chinese Broccoli.

GINGER, PRESERVED Ginger root preserved in either a clear or red sweet syrup. Sold in jars or cans in Oriental markets. Put in jar, if necessary, and store in refrigerator.

GINGER ROOT Fresh gnarled root, indispensable in Chinese cooking. Use sparingly. Very pungent and hot if used in great quantity. Young roots are available only in the spring and are more delicate and crunchy. Buy ginger root in small quantities as a little goes a long way. Store in a cool, dry place (as for potatoes and onions). A slice in cooking terms is about 1 inch in diameter and about 1/8 inch thick. There is no need to peel when mincing or thinly slicing; merely rinse.

GLUTINOUS RICE Also called sweet rice. Short-grain, opaque white rice that becomes sticky when cooked. Rich in B vitamins. Always soak at least 2 hours in cold water before cooking. Sold by weight.

GLUTINOUS RICE FLOUR Flour milled from glutinous rice. Used for dumplings and pastries. Sold in 1-pound packages.

GOLDEN NEEDLES Also called lily buds, tiger lily buds and banana flowers. Dried lily buds of the lotus flower which are pale gold in color with a delicate but distinct flavor. Always soak in cold water just until pliable (about 10 minutes) before using. Oversoaking can soften too much. Remove any hard stems after soaking. Sold packaged in plastic bags by weight in Oriental markets.

GREEN CHILI PEPPERS, HOT See Chili Peppers, Hot Green.

GROUND BEAN SAUCE See Brown Bean Sauce.

HOISIN SAUCE Thick, smooth, dark reddish brown sauce made from soybeans, spices, sugar, chili and garlic. Mildly sweet in flavor, it is used in cooking or as a condiment at the table. Available in cans. After opening, store in the refrigerator in a glass jar with a tight-fitting lid. Available in Oriental markets.

HOT BEAN PASTE Also known as hot bean sauce. Thick red chili paste made with beans, chili and spices. Available in cans and jars.

JUJUBES Also known as red dates. Dried small wrinkled red fruit similar to dates, used to flavor soups, meats, fish, poultry and sweet dishes. Imparts a subtle sweetness.

KANTEN See Agar-Agar.

LAVER See Seaweed, Dried.

LICHEE Or litchi. Canned whitish fruit about the size of a small walnut. Sweet and fragrant. Comes packed in light syrup ready to eat from the can.

LILY BUDS See Golden Needles.

LONG BEANS Foot-long, thin green beans similar in flavor to string beans. Available from spring to fall. May be prepared as for any string bean dish.

LONGANS See Dragon's Eyes.

LOP CHIANG See Chinese Sausage.

LOTUS ROOT Tan-colored, potato-like tuberous root of the water lily, with a crisp, crunchy texture. When cut, has a lacy look. Sold fresh, canned and dried. Dried lotus root is used mainly for soups and should be soaked in warm water to soften. Will expand considerably during cooking. Use only fresh or canned lotus root for stir-fry vegetable dishes.

LOTUS SEEDS Hard, brown small seeds of the lotus root. Delicate taste; used mainly as a flavoring agent in soups. Available dried or canned in Oriental markets.

MUNG BEAN SPROUTS Young sprouts of mung beans most often referred to merely as bean sprouts. Mung bean specified to distinguish from soybean sprout which is not as readily available except in Chinese markets. Fresh sprouts should be eaten within 2 to 3 days of purchasing.

NAM GOOEY See Bean-Curd Cheese, Red.

NAPA CABBAGE Also called Chinese lettuce, celery cabbage and Chinese cabbage.

Grows upright about 10 to 14 inches tall. Tightly packed, yellow to light green in color with white stalks. Available fresh all year in most markets.

NORI See Seaweed, Dried.

ORIENTAL SESAME OIL See Sesame Oil, Oriental.

OYSTER SAUCE A thick, brown sauce made of oysters, soy and brine. Imparts a rich subtle flavoring of its own. Often used as an alternative seasoning to soy sauce. May also be used as a table condiment. Good with meats, poultry, eggs and vegetables. Sold in bottles or cans in Oriental markets and some supermarkets. Store in cool place in a jar with a tight-fitting lid, or refrigerate.

OYSTERS, DRIED Brownish colored with a strong, slightly smoky scent. Must be soaked in hot water to soften, then well rinsed. Imparts a rich, pleasing taste of oysters and enriches the broth of soups and other dishes. Sold by weight in Oriental markets. Expensive, but only used sparingly.

PEPPERS, DRIED RED CHILI See Chili Peppers, Dried Red.

PEPPERS, HOT GREEN CHILI See Chili Peppers, Hot Green.

PICKLED SCALLIONS Small white bulbs of scallions pickled in vinegar and sugar. Available in jars at Oriental markets.

PLUM SAUCE Thick fruit sauce made from plums, apricots, chili, ginger, vinegar and sugar. Very similar to fruit chutney. Use as a table condiment with roast meats or poultry, especially duck, or in cooking sweet and sour dishes. Available in cans or jars. Refrigerate after opening.

PRESERVED ANCIENT EGGS See Ancient Eggs, Preserved.

PRESERVED GINGER See Ginger, Preserved.

PRESERVED SZECHWAN CABBAGE See Szechwan Cabbage, Preserved.

PRESERVED TURNIPS, CHINESE See Chinese Preserved Turnips.

PY MEI FUN See Rice-Stick Noodles.

RED CHILI PEPPERS, DRIED See Chili Peppers, Dried Red.

RED BEAN-CURD CHEESE See Bean-Curd Cheese, Red.

RED DATES See Jujubes.

RICE FLOUR Flour milled from regular rice.

RICE-STICK NOODLES (PY MEI FUN) Also called vermicelli. Dried, thin, white or opaque rice noodles. Soak in warm water 10 minutes if using for soups or stir-fried dishes. To fry: Separate into small handfuls and drop into 1/2-inch deep, hot peanut oil for a few seconds. They will immediately expand greatly. Remove and drain.

RICE STICKS (SHA HA FUN) Same as rice-stick noodles, but are wider (about 1/4 inch) and are individually coiled. Used in noodle soups or stir-fried noodle dishes. Soak in warm water before using. *Never* used for deep-frying.

RICE VINEGAR Red or white, with a milder tartness than American vinegars. Substitute red or white wine vinegar.

RICE WINE Wine made from fermented rice with a higher alcohol content than table wine. Gin or dry sherry may be substituted in most cases.

SALTED BAMBOO SHOOTS See Bamboo Shoots, Salted.

SALTED EGGS Duck eggs sometimes sold in salt brine; other times have appearance of preserved ancient eggs. The white will be liquid and cloudy, the yolk golden orange in color and slightly firm. Sold individually in Oriental markets. (See recipe, page 48.)

SALTED FISH Salted and dried fish available in cans or jars packed in oil or dried. Always scale and rinse before using. A small piece will flavor a full dish of steamed pork, so use sparingly. Available in Oriental markets.

SEAWEED, DRIED Also called laver and nori. Dark grayish-purple seaweed available in thin pressed sheets about 8 inches square (ready to use), or loose. Unpressed seaweed must be soaked to soften in warm water and washed very thoroughly to rid it of sand. Used in soup; very nutritious and high in iodine.

SESAME OIL, ORIENTAL Golden brown oil made from toasted sesame seeds. Used mainly as a flavoring for its distinctive pungent aroma and nutty taste. Use sparingly and subtly. Available in bottles at Oriental markets.

SESAME-SEED PASTE Made from ground seasame seeds. Heavy nut-like flavor similar to peanut butter. Available in jars or cans. Store in a cool place or in the refrigerator. Available in Oriental markets.

SHA HA FUN See Rice Sticks.

SHRIMP, DRIED Shelled, dried salty shrimp available in several sizes, 1/4 to 1/2 inch or 1 inch. Enriches and imparts a delicate flavor to dishes. Soak to soften and save liquid for cooking or to add to soup pot. Sold by weight in Oriental markets.

SILK MELON OR SILK SQUASH See Chinese Okra.

GLOSSARY

SMITHFIELD HAM See Virginia Ham.

SNOW PEAS Edible flat pea pod; always remove string before cooking. Requires short cooking time to retain green color and crispness. Available all year.

SOY SAUCE Made from soybeans, wheat flour, salt and sugar. Light soy sauce, also called thin soy, is topaz in color, delicate and preferred for table condiment and for use in clearer, lighter dishes. Dark soy, also called black or heavy soy, has caramel added for color and is much darker, thicker and richer in flavor than light soy. Always use sparingly. The saltiness of the soy sauce varies with the brand. Imported Oriental soy sauces are superior in flavor and quality. Japanese soy sauce is a cross between light and dark soy, is slightly sweeter than Chinese soy and may be used with good results. Available in jars or cans. Store on shelf.

STAR ANISE Dry, licorice-flavored, star-shaped seed. Used as a spice in soups, braised dishes, etc.

SWEET RICE See Glutinous Rice.

SZECHWAN CABBAGE, PRESERVED Also called Szechwan mustard pickle. Preserved in salt and red chili. Must be well rinsed or soaked if excessively salty. Available in cans. After opening, store in refrigerator.

SZECHWAN PEPPERCORNS Also called anise pepper and wild pepper. Tangy brown peppercorns or small seeds, mildly hot in taste with a pleasing pungent aroma. Sold whole by weight.

TANGERINE PEEL, DRIED Dried, orange-amber tangerine skin used as a flavoring. Adds a subtle fruit-peel taste to dishes. Use sparingly. For recipes, 1 piece is approximately 1-inch square. Always soak first in warm water to soften; then scrape off white pulp before using. Peel with a lighter skin is considered of better quality. The older the skin, the mellower the flavoring. Sold in packages by weight.

TEA MELON Amber-colored, sweet, narrow melon, about 2 to 3 inches long, belonging to the cucumber family. Available in jars or cans preserved in sweet syrup. May be eaten as is or cooked with dishes as a flavoring. Refrigerate in a jar with a tight-fitting lid.

THOUSAND-YEAR EGGS See Ancient Eggs, Preserved.

VIRGINIA HAM Also called Smithfield ham. Comes closest to duplicating the flavor of Chinese ham. Use subtly for its smoky flavor. Westphalian ham or prosciutto may be substituted, or use regular smoked ham.

WATER CHESTNUTS Walnut-size marsh plant with brown skin. Must be peeled before using. Meat is white, crisp and sweet. Canned water chestnuts come peeled and packed in water.

WILD PEPPER See Szechwan Peppercorns.

WINTER MELON Large, melon-shaped green squash with a powdery white film on skin which should always be scrubbed off well if preparing with skin left on. Remove seeds and soft pulp and discard. Melon meat is white and almost translucent when cooked. Sold whole or in pieces by the pound.

WOOD EARS Large, dried, brownish-black fungus similar to cloud ears, but considerably larger with a coarser texture. Must be soaked in warm water before using and tough ends should be removed. Sold by weight.

YELLOW BEAN SAUCE See Brown Bean Sauce.

INDEX

Abalone, Marinated, 102
Agar-Agar Salad, 84
Almond Cookies, 175
Almond Float, 176
Almond Tea, 177
Ancient Egg Diamonds, Steamed, 49
Ancient Eggs, Preserved, 47
Appetizers
    Abalone, Marinated, 102
    Ancient Egg Diamonds, Steamed, 49
    Bean Curd Salad, 57
    Beef Shui Mai, 170
    Bell Pepper or Bitter Melon Variation, Braised Stuffed, 138
    Cha Siew Bao (Steamed Buns with Pork Filling), 164
    Cold Bean-Curd Appetizer, 58
    Egg Rolls, 50
    Fried Gizzards and Livers, 135
    Fried Won Ton with Shrimp or Curried Beef Filling, 172
    Gai Bao (Steamed Buns with Chicken Filling), 165
    Golden Coin Eggs, 50
    Guon Fun (Rice Noodle Roll with Vegetables and Meat), 77
    Har Gow (Shrimp and Bamboo Shoot Filling), 168
    Hom Fun, 77
    Jao Tze, 166
    Jellied Chicken, 122
    Kuoteh or Pot Stickers (Fried Jao Tze), 167
    Mushrooms, Braised Stuffed, 138
    Mushrooms Variation, Steamed Stuffed, 138
    Peppery Clams, 101
    Pork and Shrimp Won Ton Filling, 170
    Pork, Dried Shrimp and Mushroom Fun Goh, 169
    Pork Kidney, Cucumber and Mung Bean Sprouts, 145
    Pot Stickers with Beef and Water Chestnuts, 166
    Preserved Ancient Eggs, 47
    Salted Eggs, 48
    Smoked Eggs, 48
    Shrimp and Pork Shui Mai, 171
    Shrimp Toast, 173
    Spiced Fish, 103
    Squid, Marinated, 103
    Sweet and Sour Chicken Wings, 134
    Tea Eggs, 47
Asparagus, Stir-Fried Pork with, 140

Bacon and Broccoli, Stir-Fried, 95
Bamboo Leaves, Stuffed, with Glutinous Rice, Chinese Sausage and Chestnuts, 168
Bamboo Shoots, Mushrooms and Cucumbers, 96
Bamboo Shoots, Salted, see Salted Bamboo Shoots
Bao
    Cha Siew Bao (Steamed Buns with Pork Filling), 164
    Gai Bao (Steamed Buns with Chicken Filling), 165
Barbecued Lamb, 149
Barbecued Pork (Cha Siew), 142
Barbecued Spareribs, 144

Basic Beef Stock, 34
Basic Fish Stock, 33
Basic Pork Stock, 34
Basic Rich Chicken Stock, 33
Basic Soup Noodles, 74
Basic Steamed Beef, 150
Basic Steamed Bread, 161
Basic Steamed Fish, 112
Basic Steamed Pork, 137
Basic Stir-Fried Vegetables, 89
Bean Curd
    Bean Curd and Peanut Salad, 58
    Bean Curd Casserole, 61
    Bean Curd in Earthen Pot, 61
    Bean Curd Rolls, Steamed, 63
    Bean Curd Salad, 57
    Bean Curd Soup, 42
    Bean Curd with Egg Yolks and Mixed Meats, 62
    Bean Curd with Meat and Vegetables, 61
    Bean Curd with Pork, Steamed, 62
    Braised Fish with Fried Bean Curd, 115
    Cold Bean-Curd Appetizer, 58
    Deep-Fried Bean Curd, 58
    Fermented Black Beans with Bean-Curd Cakes, 61
    Fuzzy Melon Soup with Bean Curd Variation, 37
    Ma Po Bean Curd, 59
    Mock Chicken, 62
    Pressed Bean Curd, 57
    Seaweed Soup with Bean Curd Variation, 41
    Stir-Fried Bean Curd, 59
    Stuffed Bean Curd, 60

INDEX

Bean-Thread Noodles
  Deep-Fried Bean-Thread Noodles, 73
  Duck Liver Soup with Bean-Thread Noodles Variation, 37
  Fuzzy Melon Soup with Bean-Thread Noodles Variation, 37
  Parboiling Bean-Thread Noodles, 72
  Shredded Lamb with Bean-Thread Noodles, 146
  Stirred Eggs with Bean-Thread Noodles, 54
  Szechwan Cabbage and Bean-Thread Noodle Soup, 44
Beef
  Basic Steamed Beef, 150
  Basic Steamed Beef with Chinese Preserved Turnip, 150
  Basic Steamed Beef with Preserved Szechwan Cabbage, 150
  Basic Steamed Beef with Salted Bamboo Shoots, 150
  Basic Steamed Beef with Tea Melon, 150
  Beef and Rice, 68
  Beef and Turnips in Earthen Pot, 149
  Beef Shui Mai, 171
  Curried Beef Filling for Fried Won Ton, 172
  Curried Beef Soup, 38
  Curry, Tomato and Beef Chow Mein, 78
  Egg Rolls with Meat or Poultry Variation, 50
  Jao Tze, 166
  Kuoteh or Pot Stickers (Fried Jao Tze), 167
  Mongolian Beef Variation, 148
  Mongolian Firepot, 157
  Pot Stickers with Beef and Water Chestnuts, 166
  Red-Cooked Beef Tongue, 155
  Rice Noodles with Stir-Fried Beef and Vegetables, 80
  Shredded Beef and Onions, 152
  Spiced Beef, 154
  Steak Kew, 153
  Steak Kew with Hoisin Sauce Variation, 153
  Steak Kew with Hot Bean Paste Variation, 153
  Steamed Beef with Rice Crumbs, 150
  Stir-Fried Beef with Bok Choy (Chinese Chard), 151
  Stir-Fried Ginger Beef, 152
  Szechwan Beef Stew, 154

Beef Broth with Ginger, 38
Beef Broth with Ginger and Soybean Sprouts or Napa Cabbage Variation, 38
Beef Stock, Basic, 34
Bell Pepper Variation, Braised Stuffed, 138
Bitter Melon Variation, Braised Stuffed, 138
Black Bean Sauce, Basic Stir-Fry Crab with, 111
Black Bean Sauce, Clams with, 109
Black Bean Sauce, Oysters with, 107
Black Bean Sauce, Stir-Fried Vegetables with, 90
Bok Choy (Chinese Chard), Stir-Fried Beef with, 151
Brains Foo Yung, 52
Bread, Basic Steamed, 161
Broccoli and Bacon, Stir-Fried, 95
Broccoli, Stir-Fried Fish Fillet with, 115
Brown Bean Sauce, Basic Steamed Fish with, 112
Brown Bean Sauce, Basic Stir-Fry Crab with, 111
Brown Bean Sauce, Stir-Fried Vegetables with, 90
Brown Bean Sauce, Striped Bass with, 112

Cabbage, Pork Balls and, 139
Cabbage Relish, Sour-Hot Napa, 85
Cabbage Soup, Napa, 39
Cabbage, Sweet and Sour, 87
Cabbage Variation, Beef Broth with Ginger, 38
Cantonese Fried Chicken, 127
Celestial Soup, 34
Cha Siew Bao (Steamed Buns with Pork Filling), 164
Cha Siew (Barbecued Pork), 142
Chestnuts, Braised Chicken and, 131
Chestnuts, Glutinous Rice and Chinese Sausage, Stuffed Bamboo Leaves with, 168
Chicken
  Bean Curd Casserole, 61
  Bean Curd with Meat and Vegetables, 61
  Braised Chicken and Chestnuts, 131
  Braised Chicken with Golden Needles, 131
  Braised Chicken with Oyster Sauce, 133
  Cantonese Fried Chicken, 127
  Chicken and Corn Soup, 39
  Chicken and Ham Foo Yung, 53
  Chicken and Peanuts with Chili Peppers, 130
  Chicken and Vegetables, 132

  Chicken Livers and Cucumbers, 135
  Chicken, Mushroom, Bamboo Shoots and Rice, 69
  Chicken with Dried Forest Mushrooms, 133
  Chicken with Nuts and Vegetables, 134
  Cold Noodles with Chicken and Peanuts, 76
  Crispy Chicken, 125
  Drunken Chicken, 123
  Egg Rolls Variation, 50
  Eight-Flavored Shredded Chicken, 132
  Fried Gizzards and Livers, 135
  Gai Bao (Steamed Buns with Chicken Filling), 165
  Jellied Chicken, 122
  Hot and Sweet Diced Chicken, 128
  Many Treasures Firepot, 157
  Pineapple Chicken, 128
  Red-Cooked Chicken in Spices, 126
  Salt Roasted Chicken, 125
  Smoked Chicken, 124
  Steamed Chicken with Rice Flour, 127
  Steamed Whole Chicken, 123
  Sweet and Sour Chicken Wings, 134
  Velvet Chicken, 126
  White Cut Chicken, 122
  Wine-Chicken Soup, 37
Chicken Stock, Basic Rich, 33
Chicken Stock, Quick, 33
Chinese Chives, Stirred Eggs and, 55
Chinese Mustard Green Pickle, 84
Chinese Pancakes, 81
Chinese Preserved Turnips, Basic Steamed Beef with, 150
Chinese Preserved Turnips, Basic Steamed Pork with, 137
Chinese Sausage and Rice, 68
Chinese Sausage, Basic Steamed Pork with, 137
Chinese Sausage, Chestnuts and Glutinous Rice, Steamed Bamboo Leaves with, 168
Chow Mein, Curry, Tomato and Beef, 78
Chow Mein (Pan-Fried Noodles), 78
Chrysanthemum Fish Soup, 35
Chrysanthemum Soup, 34
Clams, Peppery, 101
Clams, Stuffed, 108
Clams with Black Bean Sauce, 109
Cold Noodles with Chicken and Peanuts, 76
Cold Noodles with Mixed Vegetables, 76

Congee, 67
Corn and Chicken Soup, 39
Crab, Basic Stir-Fry, 110-111
Crab with Brown Bean Sauce, Basic Stir-Fry, 111
Crab with Egg Binder, Basic Stir-Fry, 111
Crab with Fermented Black Bean Sauce, Basic Stir-Fry, 111
Crabs, Steamed Live, 106
Crispy Chicken, 125
Crispy Duck, 117
Crispy Skin Roast Pork, 142
Cucumber, Mung Bean Sprouts and Pork Kidney, 145
Cucumber Relish, Spicy, 85
Cucumbers, Bamboo Shoots and Mushrooms, 96
Curried Beef Filling for Won Ton, 172
Curried Beef Soup, 38
Curried Lamb Stew, 146
Curry, Tomato and Beef Chow Mein, 78
Curry-Tomato Sauce, 114
Custard, Steamed Egg, 51

Deep-Fried Bean Curd, 58
Deep-Fried Bean-Thread Noodles, 73
Deep-Fried Rice-Stick Noodles (Py Mei Fun), 73
Diced Winter Melon Soup, 37
Dim Sum
  Beef Shui Mai, 171
  Cha Siew Bao (Steamed Buns with Pork Filling), 164
  Egg Rolls, 50
  Fried Gizzards and Livers, 135
  Fried Won Ton, 172
  Gai Bao (Steamed Buns with Chicken Filling), 165
  Guon Fun (Rice Noodle Roll with Vegetables and Meat), 77
  Har Gow (Shrimp and Bamboo Shoot Filling), 168
  Hom Fun, 77
  Jao Tze, 166
  Kuoteh or Pot Stickers (Fried Jao Tze), 167
  Pork and Shrimp Shui Mai, 171
  Pork and Shrimp Won Ton Filling, 170
  Pork, Dried Shrimp and Mushroom Fun Goh, 169
  Pot Stickers with Beef and Water Chestnuts, 166
  Shrimp Toast, 173

Spring Rolls, 173
Stuffed Bamboo Leaves with Glutinous Rice, Chinese Sausage and Chestnuts, 168
Sweet and Sour Chicken Wings, 134
Dipping Sauce, 163
Doughs, see Skins and Doughs
Dragon Eye Pudding, 176
Drunken Chicken, 123
Dry-Cooked Long Beans, 94
Duck
  Crispy Duck, 117
  Duck Liver Soup, 35
  Duck with Dried Forest Mushrooms Variation, 133
  Peking Roast Duck (Simplified), 117
  Red-Cooked Duck, 119
  Roast Duck, Home Style, 118
  Salt Duck, Steamed, 120
  Tea Smoked Duck, 118
  Winter Melon and Duck Soup in Earthen Pot Variation, 36

Earthen Pot Dishes
  Bean Curd in Earthen Pot, 61
  Beef or Lamb and Turnips in Earthen Pot, 149
  Chicken with Dried Forest Mushrooms, 133
  Glutinous Rice with Ham and Dried Shrimp, 67
  Winter Melon and Duck Soup in Earthen Pot Variation, 36
  Winter Melon and Squab Soup in Earthen Pot, 36
Eggs
  Ancient Egg Diamonds, Steamed, 49
  Bean Curd with Egg Yolks and Mixed Meats, 62
  Brains Foo Yung, 52
  Chicken and Ham Foo Yung, 53
  Egg Curd Soup, 40
  Egg Custard, Steamed, 51
  Egg Meatballs on Spinach, 54
  Egg Rolls, 50
  Egg Slivers, 50
  Egg Soup, Poached, 40
  Fish Egg Foo Yung, 53
  Golden Coin Eggs, 50
  Ham, Peas, Eggs and Rice, 69
  Heavenly Egg Drop Soup, 41
  Mo Shu Ro (Mixed Vegetables with Eggs and Pork), 93
  Peking Stirred Egg Yolks, 55
  Preserved Ancient Eggs, 47
  Salted Duck Egg with Pork, Steamed, 49
  Salted Eggs, 48
  Smoked Eggs, 48

Stirred Eggs and Chinese Chives, 55
Stirred Eggs and Peas, 55
Stirred Eggs with Bean-Thread Noodles, 54
Tea Eggs, 47
Egg Drop Soup, 41
Egg Flower Tea, Sweet, 177
Egg Noodle Dough, 71
Egg Noodles, Parboiling, 71
Egg Rolls, 50
Egg Rolls with Meat or Poultry Variation, 50
Egg Slivers, 50
Eggplant, Fried, 99
Eggplant Hunan Style, 98
Eggplant, Szechwan-Style, 99
Eggplant with Peanut Butter, 87
Eight-Flavored Shredded Chicken, 132

Fermented Bean Cake or Red Bean-Curd Cheese, Basic Steamed Pork with, 137
Fermented Bean Cake, Steamed Spareribs with, 144
Fermented Bean Cake, Stir-Fried Vegetables with, 91
Fermented Black Bean Sauce, Basic Steamed Fish with, 112
Fermented Black Beans with Bean-Curd Cakes, 63
Firepot Cooking, 156
  Many Treasures Firepot, 157
  Mongolian Firepot, 157
Fish and Shellfish
  Abalone, Marinated, 102
  Basic Steamed Fish, 112
  Basic Steamed Fish with Brown Bean Sauce, 112
  Basic Steamed Fish with Fermented Black Bean Sauce, 112
  Basic Steamed Fish with Forest Mushrooms, 112
  Braised Fish with Fried Bean Curd, 115
  Chrysanthemum Fish Soup, 35
  Clams, Peppery, 101
  Clams, Stuffed, 108
  Clams with Black Bean Sauce, 109
  Crab, Basic Stir-Fry, 110-111
  Crab with Brown Bean Sauce, Basic Stir-Fry, 111
  Crab with Egg Binder, Basic Stir-Fry, 111
  Crab with Fermented Black Bean Sauce, Basic Stir-Fry, 111
  Crabs, Steamed Live, 106
  Dried Shrimp, Pork and Mushroom Fun Goh, 169

INDEX

Egg Rolls, 50
Fish Ball Soup Variation, 41
Fish Egg Foo Yung, 53
Glutinous Rice with Ham and Dried Shrimp, 67
Har Gow (Shrimp and Bamboo Shoot Filling), 168
Hot and Sour Fish Soup, 44
Many Treasures Firepot, 157
Oyster Salad, 101
Oyster Soup, 42
Oysters with Black Bean Sauce, 107
Phoenix Tail Prawns and Snow Peas, 104
Prawns in their Shells, Stir-Fry, 108
Raw Fish and Noodle Salad, 102
Scallop Ball Soup Variation, 41
Shrimp and Pork Shui Mai, 171
Shrimp and Pork Won Ton Filling, 170
Shrimp Ball Soup, 41
Shrimp Filling for Fried Won Ton, 173
Shrimp in Hot and Sour Sauce, 105
Shrimp Toast, 173
Spiced Fish, 103
Squid, Marinated, 103
Squid, Sweet and Sour, 111
Stir-Fried Fish Fillet with Broccoli, 115
Striped Bass with Brown Bean Sauce, 112
Whole Fried Fish, 114
Whole Poached Fish, 113
Fish Stock, Basic, 33
Five-Treasure Vegetable Stir-Fry, 92
Foo Yung
    Brains Foo Yung, 52
    Chicken and Ham Foo Yung, 53
    Fish Egg Foo Yung, 53
Forest Mushrooms, Basic Steamed Fish with, 112
Forest Mushrooms, Basic Steamed Pork with, 137
Forest Mushrooms, Dried, Chicken with, 133
Forest Mushrooms Variation, Dried, Duck with, 133
Forest Mushrooms Variation, Dried, Squab with, 133
Fried Chicken, Cantonese, 127
Fried Fish, Whole, 114
Fried Jao Tze (Kuoteh or Pot Stickers), 167
Fried Rice, Pork, 66
Fried Won Ton, 172
Fruit Puffs, Fried, 177
Fruit Sweet and Sour Sauce, 141
Fun Goh Dough, 162

Fun Goh, Pork, Dried Shrimp and Mushroom, 169
Fun, Homemade, 72
Fuzzy Melon Soup, 37
Fuzzy Melon Soup with Bean Curd Variation, 37
Fuzzy Melon Soup with Bean-Thread Noodles Variation, 37

Garlic, Minced, Pork with, 143
Ginger Beef Broth, 38
Ginger Beef Broth with Soybean Sprouts or Napa Cabbage Variation, 38
Ginger Beef, Stir-Fried, 152
Ginger Lemon Sauce, 107
Gizzards and Livers, Fried, 152
Glutinous Rice, Steamed, 65
Glutinous Rice, Chinese Sausage and Chestnuts, Stuffed Bamboo Leaves with, 168
Glutinous Rice with Ham and Dried Shrimp, 67
Golden Coin Eggs, 50
Golden Needles, Braised Chicken with, 131
Green Onion Pancakes, 81
Green Onion Sauce, 107
Guon Fun (Rice Noodle Roll with Meat and Vegetables), 77

Ham and Chicken Foo Yung, 53
Ham, Basic Steamed Pork with, 137
Ham, Peas, Eggs and Rice, 69
Har Gow (Shrimp and Bamboo Shoot Filling), 168
Heavenly Egg Drop Soup, 41
High Moisture-Content Vegetables and Cutting Methods, 88
Hoisin Sauce, Stir-Fried Vegetables with, 92
Hoisin Sauce Variation, Steak Kew with, 153
Hom Fun, 77
Homemade Fun, 72
Hot and Sour Fish Soup, 44
Hot and Sour Soup, 45
Hot and Sweet Diced Chicken, 128
Hot Bean Paste Variation, Steak Kew with, 153

Iceberg Lettuce Soup, 39

Jao Tze, 166
Jao Tze Dough, 161
Jao Tze, Fried (Kuoteh or Pot Stickers), 167
Jellied Chicken, 122
Jook, 67

Kidney, Pork, Mung Bean Sprouts and Cucumber, 145
Kuoteh or Pot Stickers (Fried Jao Tze), 167

Lamb
    Barbecued Lamb, 149
    Curried Lamb Stew, 146
    Egg Rolls Variation, 50
    Lamb and Turnips in Earthen Pot, 149
    Mongolian Firepot, 157
    Mongolian Grill, 148
    Mongolian Lamb, 148
    Shredded Lamb with Bean-Thread Noodles, 146
Liver Soup, Duck or Chicken, 35
Liver Soup Variation, Duck or Chicken with Bean-Thread Noodles, 35
Livers and Gizzards, Fried, 135
Livers, Chicken, and Cucumbers, 135
Long Beans, Dry-Cooked, 94
Long Life Noodles, 79
Lotus Root, Marinated, 86
Low Moisture-Content Vegetables and Cutting Methods, 88

Ma Po Bean Curd, 59
Many Treasures Firepot, 157
Meatballs, Egg, on Spinach, 54
Mixed Vegetable Pickle, 83
Mixed Vegetables with Eggs and Pork, 93
Mo Shu Ro, 93
Mock Chicken, 62
Mock Fish, 97
Mongolian Beef Variation, 148
Mongolian Firepot, 157
Mongolian Grill, 148
Mongolian Lamb, 148
Mung Bean Sprout and Sparerib Soup, 37
Mung Bean Sprout Salad, 84
Mung Bean Sprouts, Cucumber and Pork Kidney, 145
Mushrooms, Braised Stuffed, 138
Mushrooms, Cucumbers and Bamboo Shoots, 96
Mushrooms, Pork and Dried Shrimp Fun Goh, 169
Mushrooms Variation, Steamed Stuffed, 138
Mustard Green Pickle, Chinese, 84
Mustard Greens Soup, 38

Napa Cabbage, Pork Balls and, 139
Napa Cabbage Relish, Sour-Hot, 85
Napa Cabbage Soup, 39
Napa Cabbage Variation, Beef Broth with Ginger and, 38

Noodles and Noodle Dishes
Chow Mein (Pan-Fried Noodles), 78
Cold Noodles with Chicken and Peanuts, 76
Cold Noodles with Mixed Vegetables, 76
Curry, Tomato and Beef Chow Mein, 78
Deep-Fried Bean-Thread Noodles, 73
Deep-Fried Rice-Stick Noodles (Py Mei Fun), 73
Duck Liver Soup with Bean-Thread Noodles Variation, 35
Egg Noodle Dough, 71
Fuzzy Melon Soup with Bean-Thread Noodles Variation, 37
Guon Fun (Rice Noodle Roll with Meat and Vegetables), 77
Homemade Fun, 72
Long Life Noodles, 79
Minced Squab and Fried Rice Noodles, 121
Pan-Fried Rice Noodles, 73
Parboiling Bean-Thread Noodles, 72
Parboiling Egg Noodles, 71
Parboiling Rice Noodles, 72
Parboiling Wheat Noodles, 71
Raw Fish and Noodle Salad, 102
Rice Noodle Skins, 72
Rice Noodles with Stir-Fried Beef and Vegetables, 80
Shredded Lamb with Bean-Thread Noodles, 54
Soup Noodles, Basic, 74
Soup Noodles with Treasures from the Sea, 74
Stirred Eggs with Bean-Thread Noodles, 54
Szechwan Cabbage and Bean-Thread Noodles, 44
Won Ton Soup, Basic, 74
Won Ton Soup with Barbecued Pork Variation, 75
Won Ton Soup with Beef Variation, 75

Onions, Shredded Beef and, 152
Oyster Salad, 101
Oyster Sauce, Braised Chicken with, 133
Oyster Soup, 42
Oysters with Black Bean Sauce, 107

Pan-Fried Noodles (Chow Mein), 78
Pan-Fried Rice Noodles, 73
Pancakes, Chinese, 81
Pancakes, Green Onion, 81
Peanut and Bean Curd Salad, 58
Peanuts and Chicken with Chili Peppers, 130
Peas, Stirred Eggs and, 55
Peking Roast Duck (Simplified), 117
Peking Stirred Egg Yolks, 55
Peppers and Walnuts in Sweet and Sour Sauce, 94
Phoenix Tail Prawns and Snow Peas, 104
Pickled Vegetables, see Relishes and Salads
Pineapple Chicken, 128
Pork
Barbecued Pork (Cha Siew), 142
Barbecued Spareribs, 144
Basic Steamed Pork, 137
Basic Steamed Pork with Chinese Preserved Turnip, 137
Basic Steamed Pork with Fermented Bean Cake or Red Bean-Curd Cheese, 137
Basic Steamed Pork with Forest Mushrooms, 137
Basic Steamed Pork with Ham or Chinese Sausage, 137
Basic Steamed Pork with Preserved Szechwan Cabbage, 137
Basic Steamed Pork with Salt Fish, 137
Basic Steamed Pork with Salted Bamboo Shoots, 137
Bean Curd with Pork, Steamed, 62
Braised Stuffed Bell Pepper or Bitter Melon, 138
Braised Stuffed Mushrooms, 138
Cha Siew Bao (Steamed Buns with Pork Filling), 164
Cha Siew (Barbecued Pork), 142
Crispy Skin Roast Pork, 142
Egg Meatballs on Spinach, 54
Ham and Chicken Foo Yung, 53
Ham, Peas, Eggs and Rice, 69
Jao Tze, 166
Kuoteh or Pot Stickers (Fried Jao Tze), 167
Long Life Noodles, 79
Ma Po Bean Curd, 59
Many Treasures Firepot, 157
Mo Shu Ro (Mixed Vegetables with Eggs and Pork), 93
Pork and Shrimp Shui Mai, 171
Pork and Shrimp Won Ton Filling, 170

Pork and Turnip Soup, 38
Pork Balls and Cabbage, 139
Pork, Dried Shrimp and Mushroom Fun Goh, 169
Pork Fried Rice, 66
Pork Kidney, Cucumbers and Mung Bean Sprouts, 145
Salted Duck Egg with Pork, Steamed, 49
Sparerib and Mung Bean Sprout Soup, 37
Spareribs, Barbecued, 144
Spareribs with Three Sauces, Steamed, 144
Stuffed Mushrooms Variation, Steamed, 138
Stir-Fried Pork with Asparagus, 140
Sweet and Sour Pork, 141
Twice-Cooked Pork, 143
Pork Stock, Basic, 34
Pork Stock, Quick, 34
Pot Stickers or Kuoteh (Fried Jao Tze), 167
Pot Stickers with Beef and Water Chestnuts, 166
Prawns, Phoenix Tail, and Snow Peas, 104
Prawns in their Shells, Stir-Fry, 108
Preserved Ancient Eggs, 47
Preserved Szechwan Cabbage and Bean-Thread Noodle Soup, 44
Preserved Szechwan Cabbage, Basic Steamed Beef with, 150
Preserved Szechwan Cabbage, Basic Steamed Pork with, 137
Pressed Bean Curd, 57

Quick Chicken Stock, 33
Quick Pork Stock, 34

Red-Cooked Beef Tongue, 155
Red-Cooked Chicken in Spices, 126
Red-Cooked Duck, 119
Relishes and Salads
Agar-Agar Salad, 84
Bean Curd and Peanut Salad, 58
Bean Curd Salad, 57
Chinese Mustard Green Pickle, 84
Marinated Lotus Root, 86
Mixed Vegetable Pickle, 83
Mung Bean Sprout Salad, 84
Oyster Salad, 101
Raw Fish and Noodle Salad, 102
Sour-Hot Napa Cabbage Relish, 85
Spicy Cucumber Relish, 85
Sweet Pickled Vegetables, 83
White Turnip Pickle, 84

INDEX

Rice
  Beef and Rice, 68
  Chicken, Mushroom, Bamboo
    Shoots and Rice, 69
  Congee, 67
  Glutinous Rice, Steamed, 65
  Glutinous Rice with Ham and
    Dried Shrimp, 67
  Ham, Peas, Eggs and Rice, 69
  Pork Fried Rice, 66
  Reheating Rice, 65
  Rice Crumbs, 150
  Steamed Rice, 65
  Stuffed Bamboo Leaves with
    Glutinous Rice, Chinese
    Sausage and Chestnuts,
    168
Rice Noodle Roll with Vegetables
  and Meat (Guon Fun), 77
Rice Noodle Skins, 72
Rice Noodles, Pan-Fried, 73
Rice Noodles, Parboiling, 72
Rice-Stick Noodles, Fried, Minced
  Squab and, 121
Rice-Stick Noodles (Py Mei Fun),
  Deep-Fried, 73
Rice-Stick Noodles with Stir-Fried
  Beef and Vegetables, 80
Roast Duck, Home Style, 118
Roast Duck (Simplified), Peking,
  117
Roast Pork, Crispy Skin, 142

Salads, see Relishes and Salads
Salt Duck, Steamed, 120
Salt Fish, Basic Steamed Pork with,
  137
Salt Roasted Chicken, 125
Salted Bamboo Shoots, Basic
  Steamed Beef with, 150
Salted Bamboo Shoots, Basic
  Steamed Pork with, 137
Salted Duck Egg with Pork,
  Steamed, 49
Salted Eggs, 48
Sauces
  Curry-Tomato Sauce, 114
  Dipping Sauce, 163
  Fruit Sweet and Sour Sauce, 141
  Ginger Lemon Sauce, 107
  Green Onion Sauce, 107
  Sweet and Sour Sauce, 114
Scallop Ball Soup Variation, 41
Seafood, see Fish and Shellfish
Seaweed Soup, 41
Seaweed Soup with Bean Curd Var-
  iation, 41
Sesame Seed Cookies, 176
Shellfish, see Fish and Shellfish

Shrimp and Bamboo Shoot Filling
  (Har Gow), 168
Shrimp and Pork Shui Mai, 171
Shrimp and Pork Won Ton Filling,
  170
Shrimp Ball Soup, 41
Shrimp, Dried, Pork and Mushroom
  Fun Goh, 167
Shrimp Filling for Fried Won Ton,
  172
Shrimp in Hot and Sour Sauce, 105
Shrimp Toast, 173
Shui Mai
  Beef Shui Mai, 171
  Pork and Shrimp Shui Mai, 171
Sizzling Rice Soup, 43
Sizzling Rice with Shrimp in Hot
  and Sour Sauce Variation, 105
Skins and Doughs
  Basic Steamed Bread, 161
  Egg Noodle Dough, 71
  Fun Goh Dough, 162
  Jao Tze Dough, 161
  Rice Noodle Skins, 72
  Spring Roll Skins, 162
  Won Ton Dough, 163
Smoked Chicken, 124
Smoked Eggs, 48
Snow Peas, Phoenix Tail Prawns
  and, 104
Soup Noodles, Basic, 74
Soup Noodles with Treasures from
  the Sea, 74
Soups
  Basic Soup Noodles, 74
  Bean Curd Soup, 42
  Celestial Soup, 34
  Chicken and Corn Soup, 39
  Chrysanthemum Fish Soup, 35
  Chrysanthemum Soup, 34
  Congee, 67
  Curried Beef Soup, 38
  Duck Liver Soup, 34
  Duck Liver Soup, 35
  Duck Liver Soup with Bean-
    Thread Noodles Variation,
    35
  Egg Curd Soup, 40
  Egg Drop Soup, 41
  Egg Soup, Poached, 40
  Fish Ball Soup Variation, 41
  Fuzzy Melon Soup, 37
  Fuzzy Melon Soup with Bean
    Curd Variation, 37
  Fuzzy Melon Soup with Bean-
    Thread Noodles Variation,
    37
  Ginger Beef Broth, 38
  Ginger Beef Broth with Napa
    Cabbage or Soybean
    Sprouts Variation, 38

Heavenly Egg Drop Soup, 41
Hot and Sour Fish Soup, 44
Hot and Sour Soup, 45
Mustard Greens Soup, 38
Napa Cabbage Soup, 39
Oyster Soup, 42
Pork and Turnip Soup, 38
Scallop Ball Soup Variation, 41
Seaweed Soup, 41
Seaweed Soup with Bean Curd
  Variation, 41
Shrimp Ball Soup, 41
Sizzling Rice Soup, 43
Soup Noodles with Treasures
  from the Sea, 74
Sparerib and Mung Bean Sprout
  Soup, 37
Spinach Soup Variation, 38
Szechwan Cabbage and Bean-
  Thread Noodle Soup, 44
Watercress Soup Variation, 38
Wine-Chicken Soup, 37
Winter Melon and Duck Soup in
  Earthen Pot Variation, 36
Winter Melon and Squab Soup in
  Earthen Pot, 36
Winter Melon Soup, Diced, 37
Won Ton Soup, Basic, 75
Won Ton Soup with Barbecued
  Pork Variation, 75
Won Ton Soup with Beef Varia-
  tion, 75
Sour-Hot Napa Cabbage Relish, 85
Soybean Sprouts, Beef Broth with
  Ginger and, 38
Soybean Sprouts, Braised, 96
Sparerib and Mung Bean Sprout
  Soup, 37
Spareribs, Barbecued, 144
Spareribs with Fermented Bean
  Cake, Steamed, 144
Spareribs with Three Sauces,
  Steamed, 144
Spiced Beef, 154
Spiced Fish, 103
Spiced Salt, 118
Spicy Cucumber Relish, 85
Spinach, Peking Style, 97
Spinach Soup Variation, 38
Sponge Cake, Steamed, 175
Spring Roll Skins, 162
Spring Rolls, 173
Squab
  Fried Squab, 120
  Minced Squab and Fried Rice-
    Stick Noodles, 121
  Squab with Dried Forest Mush-
    rooms Variation, 133
  Winter Melon and Squab Soup
    in Earthen Pot, 36

Squid, Marinated, 103
Squid, Sweet and Sour, 111
Steak Kew, 153
Steak Kew with Hoisin Sauce Variation, 153
Steak Kew with Hot Bean Paste Variation, 153
Steamed Beef, Basic, see Beef
Steamed Beef with Rice Crumbs, 150
Steamed Chicken with Rice Flour, 127
Steamed Fish, Basic, see Fish and Shellfish
Steamed Glutinous Rice, 65
Steamed Pork, Basic, see Pork
Steamed Rice, 65
Steamed Whole Chicken, 123
Stir-Fried Bean Curd, 59
Stir-Fried Beef with Bok Choy (Chinese Chard), 151
Stir-Fried Broccoli and Bacon, 95
Stir-Fried Fish Fillet with Broccoli, 115
Stir-Fried Ginger Beef, 152
Stir-Fried Pork with Asparagus, 140
Stir-Fried Vegetables, Basic, 89
Stir-Fried Vegetables with Black Bean Sauce, 90
Stir-Fried Vegetables with Fermented Bean Cake, 91
Stir-Fried Vegetables with Hoisin Sauce, 92
Stirred Eggs and Chinese Chives, 55
Stirred Eggs and Peas, 55
Stirred Eggs with Bean-Thread Noodles, 54
Stirred Egg Yolks, Peking, 55
Stocks
    Basic Beef Stock, 34
    Basic Fish Stock, 33
    Basic Pork Stock, 34
    Basic Rich Chicken Stock, 33
    Quick Chicken Stock, 33
    Quick Pork Stock, 34
Striped Bass with Brown Bean Sauce, 112
Stuffed Bean Curd, 60
Sweet and Sour Cabbage, 87
Sweet and Sour Chicken Wings, 134
Sweet and Sour Pork, 141
Sweet and Sour Sauce, 114
Sweet and Sour Sauce, Fruit, 141
Sweet Egg Flower Tea, 177
Sweet Pickled Vegetables, 83

Sweets
    Almond Cookies, 175
    Almond Float, 176
    Almond Tea, 177
    Dragon Eye Pudding, 176
    Fried Fruit Puffs, 177
    Sesame Seed Cookies, 176
    Steamed Sponge Cake, 175
    Sweet Egg Flower Tea, 177
    Water Chestnut Pudding, 176
Szechwan Beef Stew, 154
Szechwan Cabbage and Bean-Thread Noodle Soup, 44
Szechwan Cabbage, Preserved, Basic Steamed Beef with, 150
Szechwan Cabbage, Preserved, Basic Steamed Pork with, 137

Tea Eggs, 47
Tea Melon, Basic Steamed Beef with, 150
Tea-Smoked Duck, 118
Tomato, Curry and Beef Chow Mein, 78
Tongue, Red-Cooked Beef, 155
Twice-Cooked Pork, 143
Turnip and Pork Soup, 38
Turnip Pickle, White, 84
Turnips and Lamb or Beef in Earthen Pot, 149

Vegetable Dishes
    Bamboo Shoots, Mushrooms and Cucumbers, 96
    Basic Stir-Fried Vegetables, 89
    Braised Soybean Sprouts, 96
    Cold Noodles with Mixed Vegetables, 76
    Dry-Cooked Long Beans, 94
    Eggplant Hunan Style, 98
    Eggplant with Peanut Butter, 87
    Five-Treasure Vegetable Stir-Fry, 92
    Fried Eggplant, 99
    Guon Fun, 77
    High Moisture-Content Vegetables and Cutting Methods, 88-89
    Low Moisture-Content Vegetables and Cutting Methods, 88
    Mixed Vegetables with Eggs and Pork, 93
    Mo Shu Ro, 93
    Mock Fish, 97
    Spinach, Peking Style, 97
    Stir-Fried Broccoli and Bacon, 95
    Stir-Fried Vegetables, 88
    Stir-Fried Vegetables with Black Bean Sauce, 90

Stir-Fried Vegetables with Brown Bean Sauce, 90
Stir-Fried Vegetables with Fermented Bean Cake, 91
Stir-Fried Vegetables with Hoisin Sauce, 92
Sweet and Sour Cabbage, 87
Szechwan-Style Eggplant, 99
Walnuts and Peppers in Sweet and Sour Sauce, 94
Vegetables and Chicken, 132
Vegetables, Cold
    Agar-Agar Salad, 84
    Eggplant with Peanut Butter, 87
    Marinated Lotus Root, 86
    Mixed Vegetable Pickle, 83
    Mung Bean Sprout Salad, 84
    Sour-Hot Napa Cabbage Relish, 85
    Spicy Cucumber Relish, 85
    Sweet and Sour Cabbage, 87
    Sweet Pickled Vegetables, 83
    White Turnip Pickle, 84
Vegetables, Chicken with Nuts and, 134
Velvet Chicken, 126

Walnuts and Peppers in Sweet and Sour Sauce, 94
Water Chestnut Pudding, 176
Water Chestnuts, Pot Stickers with Beef and, 166
Watercress Soup Variation, 38
Wheat Noodles, Parboiling, 71
White Cut Chicken, 122
White Turnip Pickle, 84
Whole Fried Fish, 114
Whole Poached Fish, 113
Wine-Chicken Soup, 37
Winter Melon and Duck Soup in Earthen Pot Variation, 36
Winter Melon and Squab Soup in Earthen Pot, 36
Winter Melon Soup, Diced, 37
Won Ton Dough, 163
Won Ton Filling, Pork and Shrimp, 170
Won Ton, Fried, with Curried Beef or Shrimp Filling, 172
Won Ton Soup, Basic, 75
Won Ton Soup with Barbecued Pork Variation, 75
Won Ton Soup with Beef Variation, 75

BIOGRAPHICAL NOTES

From her Cantonese ancestors Margaret Lee Gin has inherited the artful speed and impatience to cut through the intricate pedantry of classic Chinese cookery. Being also intimately acquainted with American cooking habits and food products, she is well qualified to offer a modern, simplified, economical approach to the regional foods of China. Mrs. Gin has taught Chinese cooking classes in San Francisco and is the co-author of two other 101 Productions' cookbooks: *Country Cookery of Many Lands* and *Innards and Other Variety Meats.* Another of her cookbooks, *Ricecraft,* was recently published by Yerba Buena Press.

This is Alfred Castle's second collaboration with Margaret Gin. He contributed a highly acclaimed capsule history of the world in terms of food to *Country Cookery* and now writes about how foods are woven into the fabric of China. Mr. Castle has also researched and written the historical texts for a number of other 101 cookbooks.